The Afterlife

Jason Powell
The Afterlife

Powell
England and Wales

The Afterlife
Published in 2022
by Powell Books

Tarvin Road, Chester, England, CH3 5DJ
Printed by blurb

ISBN – see cover

Contents

ARMAGEDDON

1

I was there on the day when the apocalypse happened.
I saw many ways of dying and being dead,
In a time of chaos for the people who enjoyed chaos, and for me too.
It ended in absolute nothing and loneliness, naturally.
While the worst things happened, gradually,
On the day when war destroyed all life,
There were massive casualties,
And many people not worth the trouble were killed.
I don't know who they were.
Against the laws of natural things and ways,
people had started to think in ways which deprived us of meaning.
Instead of order and rule, there was pitiless official paperwork
And where there should be love, there was disorder
And I, was waiting for the time when I would not have to struggle fruitlessly
And thinking about how I could escape
By exile or by some more drastic end of my suffering.
It was as if already, before the calamity,
already an aboriginal calamity had already made us into ghosts,
corpses, illusions, freaks who would live without the hope of resurrection.

Then, an airburst device, a nuclear bomb which splits up atoms of heavy metals
Exploded in the air at the power station and refinery in Ellesmere Port,
and all the electricity went out, all the copper wires burst into flames overloaded
All across the land.

The sky ignited in fire, the land was in a state of winter;
There was no light from the sun;
All the rivers and lakes and other water were spoiled.
My body was damaged all over in every cell.
Britain was a country between the two great enemies,
Russia and America. The Russians had been violent;
And the American politicians couldn't stop themselves,
From wanting to completely rid the world of the Russian people,
Just as they had rid the world completely of the original people of America.
I didn't want to fight or stand for my country,
Because I felt bitter about the way the community of people in England
Treated me as if I were the surplus, the accursed.

I had been a soldier, but I could not find a place in England when I came home.
The government seemed to hate me, and to prohibit men from being fathers.
So, I preferred the Russian cause.
Angry about things and wanting a new kingdom.

I prayed to Jesus, there and then, in Gresford village where I was;
I had a daughter somewhere, but she wasn't permitted to see me
I prayed to God to let me see her and take her to safety
I had made mistakes, I had done the wrong thing with my life
I should not have married the child's mother, tied myself to such a person.

That afternoon, I realised the roads would be bad
And that I would not be able to get home,
So I stayed there, working, and prayed to Jesus for peace;
I didn't want to fight; I wanted peace to see my family.
I wanted the enmity to be resolved.
I thought that in the chaos, I would go find the children and rescue them.

More than this, I wanted to think, that it was not a real problem.
So I worked on, at my labour.
But later in the day a missile landed in Liverpool,
A ground device which raised a huge cloud of fire,
Rising for miles above the land, in the colours of a rainbow,
And set most things on fire, killing everyone.
The cloud rose slowly through the sky, and blotted out the sun forever.

I thought of getting the car and going to get my children,
Then on to the sea, or up the mountains around Tanygrisiau,
And the caves there. That was my idea. I would pick up Galya on the way.
On that day, I was at work, outside near the old church, in the town where I grew up.
I was there by coincidence; I might have been anywhere else,
Outdoors with the van full of tools, on my own as usual.
While I was walking to the van, showers of white ash fell like snow.
A man came toward me through the ashes and little flames.
He wore a working man's clothes, trousers with bandages around the knees, and a thick jacket,
He looked like a hard man with a heavy head on a strong neck, and his eyes

Were slits watching me intently, hard under a furrowed brow.

"The fight is over now, it is all over now
The life is over. I come for you, and you only.
Your wife asked me to come, so that you could see her and your children again.
Everyone you knew is now gone, dead, hidden away."

He spoke in a loud voice against the winds which started blowing
While the nuclear storm cloud rose from the north behind him.
I wept. "It would have been right to fight with your old battalion.
Even though the war ended everything. For struggle and blindness
And doing bad things for the right reason
Is the lot of people who have knowledge and not enough knowledge.
It is the end. We'll make our way now."
It was dark, and we made our way through the shattered buildings and the fires.

2

I went along with him. He looked used to being in the company of people
Who have lived in troubled times and unhappy circles.
I asked: "Who are you, and where do you come from?"
"I am no body", he said.
But as the light of the explosion disappeared, mist and smoke came towards us
And the outline of a town or even a city.
I suppose it could have been like London, or Paris,
Certainly not the little village where I had grown up.
There was a wall and an arch, with the gates removed by the blast
And yet, inside, this evidence of human industry and habitation was untouched
by devastation
Though it was difficult to see through the smoke.
As we went through, my companion looked as unconcerned and confident
As Lawrence, of Arabia, sauntering into Jerusalem,
Liberating it for Christians after fifteen centuries
Easily, scruffily, as if he owned the place.

Before our eyes, the dead, the recent dead, were strewn around on the floor
And here and there, were empty holes in the concrete where
Long dead thrown up corpses had apparently got out of the ground

The air was foul with the smell of rotting things

Before me, all was in fact in motion, because these wide streets we went down
They were the big imperial building projects
From times when Englishmen had built things
To express their importance and wealth, as the Romans had done,
And vying with each other.
The town was moving, rising, falling; little by little shifting,
Eventually shrinking and declining. Evidence of recent history,
Castles, transport, machines, they were all arising and then collapsing.

I said then: "I realise now, that I myself have not survived.
Is this life after death? And who are you?
I feel that I am alone, here, alive.
This is not how reality behaves, the laws of nature are not working as they used
to."

And he replied: "You know who I am.
Who else survives death and awaits you at the apocalypse,
And brings you to judgement, and new life?"
But realising that he was Christ, or God, did not console me,
Hardly changed my feelings at all.
"I'm not happy. I have been rescued at the end of the world.
I don't understand why."

I fell to the ground, like somebody who wants to be a ghost or a zombie himself,
Like one of those people who had left their graves around us.
"We are going through all time and space
Back to the origin of Being.
I am taking you to your wife, and your children.
See the light in the sky, an unnaturally bright light
Through the smoke and the burning atmosphere;
That is the moving of the sun around from West to East,
Cycling so fast you can only discern a line of bright light
Mixing into the afterglow of days and years
That are marked by the fast cycling of the sun
Across the sky and beyond the horizon.
It's not the end. There are centuries and millenniums of collapse ahead.
The past is all ahead of us, plainly to be seen."
I touched the coat he was wearing abjectly,
Like the woman cursed with bleeding.
"Did you say you're taking me to my children and wife?
Did they survive?" He did not answer.

"You don't feel as God feels, as I feel. You feel dejected, and lonely.
Let me try to put you in the proper frame of mind for our journey."
He spoke to me then a story, just as he is reputed in the Gospels,
To have told stories to the people, and to children
With some warmth and enthusiasm, without malice, wanting me to understand:

"The church where you went, near Liverpool,
Was the home of St Elizabeth, wife of Alexander II,
Governor of Moscow, conservative archduke.
When her husband was attacked by nihilists,
Political types with bombs, while he was in a Moscow street,

Elizabeth calmly picked up her husband's body parts from the street,
Gathering them together where they lay.
Afterwards, she devoted her life to the poor, and became a nun.
During the civil war in Russia, she was imprisoned
And then buried alive down a well shaft,
Because of her devotion to God and to me.
And remember your own saint and protector, Nicholas,
Who went to Japan first among the Russians,
To announce the truth to them.
He brought fifty thousand people into the Church;
His first baptism was a of a man of the samurai order,
To whom he was able to show the way, the way of God and man.
This is how it is meant to be. The one who came to kill him,
That warrior samurai, was the first of the people to be baptised in peace.
You will be the son of God, if you can stay with me to the end. Now follow me
With all your heart, mind, and all your strength.
Come and see."

3

Here are the dead ones; shades run around the streets. I thought at the time
That maybe two hours or so had passed; by my watch, it was two hours.
And yet, by my eye I could tell, that I was in the village outside Chester still,
but maybe two thousand years had passed.
Romans and their imperial remains were scattered about;
Came out of the mist and swamp at my feet, for a while,
And then they, too, gone;
There were shades loitering around in the stones and columns
They lasted for moments, lived, then died.
But in the meantime, I asked: "All of the spaces which were in previous times
Are being revived step by step, backwards. Are we travellers in time?"
And he said: "All time and space are in the mind of the creator;
all people; all their individuality and fate are in his mind.
It is all still existing, still there, out there, beyond your sight,
because you only see a slice of things, depending on the point of time you are at.
The future, no, that doesn't exist yet. But the past, yes.
My father is now drawing it all up, like a scroll, like an architect's drawing being
rolled up.
The father and I are one; just as laboriously as I created it, from love, now to
save you from it
Also out of love, I take it apart, and dispose of it."
"What is it?" I said. "It is the earth", he replied.
"But where will everyone live, where will they all go
When the earth has been rolled up? Where will my children and my wife, and
me;
Where will we live? You did say, that I was going to see them."

"To engage in science fiction, in fantasies of literature derived from science;
It would be possible for God to do all things, any thing for you,
To bring them to you in a dream; to make a world anew just for you;
To keep a patch of this world worth living in, just for you
And people it with automata, simulacra, unreal animals and people
For your company. But God does not work with bits, fragments, illusions.
The world and the earth are real, and all that you had; what seemed and
appeared
Was and is real.
There will be a place and time for new life

But not alongside this time and place, not alongside it
Like a split universe. There is one world, real, incontrovertible, true, factual.
First, let us see the whole of creation and all knowledge, and then see where we
will go after that
And where we shall find your loved ones."

I observed among the dull noise the earth being forced back in time
And the rain which was falling by then, which was still falling from a dust filled
sky
In a dirty rain, which caused the green things to wither, and a burning on the
skin,
People tending to gather, like sheep on a Welsh hillside,
Roaming here and there in flocks.
It caused me some regret to see the people of England like this
Without their history, or their homes and towns.
They have so much trust and now have nothing to trust in.

All the people who had ever been born were now pouring out from the ground,
layer
On layer of sediment and graves, all the humans only.
No animals, and no particular resurrection of the plants either.
Just the people. But, because there were no distractions, and because
There was no order and regularity for them to cling to
They were deeply distressed, moaning, among the acrid smell and the rain.
But, angry and disappointed with people and with God, as it maybe I had been
turned,
I felt no sympathy for them.

There was a shape, however, leading, calling them together like a shepherd.
He was human, not some demonic shape with a whip and horns, not some
mythical creature.
But I knew very well who he was, because his story and his picture had been
Impressed on my mind and memory at earliest childhood in school
In Mynedd Isa, near Mold, where first I learned of the Christian man and the
British.
It was Dr David Livingstone, the explorer and solitary in this vast waste.
I knew who it was.
We were no longer, Christ and I, my master and me, in any familiar place,
But now entering onto a world beyond the counting of years; I could not guess

what era was now being rolled up and put away.
Or, the place. But that was him, the evangelist of God to the centre of darkest
Africa.

"Awake, wake up," he said to them, roughly. "Did you think that death was
more than a sleep?
Half of us sought in death an escape!
But, God has plans for you, and has awoken you
Like on an old Victorian Christmas morning, for a feast
And for gifts. Who amongst you is selfish enough, has responsibility for himself
enough
To come forward and be chosen, to go onward across this point?
Who has it in him, to recognise his own actions; to know the evil that he did
The good that he did, and own them as his?
Come on, and come through this gate.
It's a long way; difficult. Who is coming?"
Not many were willing to go the way he was pointing.
To me, it looked like he was pointing into the indefinite distance of some
mountain range
Still covered with smog and radioactive dust, and charred dead things.
Christ said to me, "We should not interrupt his work;
He is sifting out those souls, those bodies
On whom God has looked and worked, and who have got used to confessing
And not running away from their self or their maker".
However, this explorer, who had made himself without human help
But with divine angelic help if any, noticed my master
And came running over. His feet made splashes and noise through the mud
As he came; he held out his hands, so as to take my master's hand in his to kiss
it,
Bowed low. He said nothing, but looked for a moment,
Then went back to his work on the little rise among the thousands and
thousands of people.

4

We had to follow after Livingstone, and through the gate he pointed to.
There was a path going alongside a great river which ran into the sea.
We were breaking away from civilisation, land, peoples, nations
Like that river. There was a kind of boat.
At the port, standing around waiting on the shore.
Like homeless men around a fire, warming their hands in the dark
Were men, past whom we walked, who had understood God.
They turned their heads to me, as I approached, and welcomed me among them.
My master and I warmed our hands on the fire.
"These men here are Isaiah, and Jeremiah, and Amos –
The voice of God to the people. Men who heard and saw
The law and the voice of the creator.
The prophets are going ahead of everyone, and we are, too," he said.
The men said nothing to me; but they moved when my master and I did
At the call of the pilot and captain, when the boat was ready.

I think we were now set loose of all land and all safety,
Entering into the complete dissolution
But safe in the walls of that transport.

"Why did they not see you with me?" I asked.
"Livingstone was able to see you; why not those leaders of the Jews".
"Rather," he said, "ask do you think that I am spending time only with you?
I am with others, with other men, also. I am with them already.
But, there are things here which only you see.
This is your life only, this is your death alone.
The gate you passed and the law of right and evil,
Where evil and the good are weighed – is your gate.
That gate which you just came through: that is yours alone.
Perhaps, I am not here for you only.
But, I am going to look after you; be resolute, by happy; I am here."

On the boat we got. A ship with a sail.
"When we land, on the other shore, any space will be timely.
Any movement we make will take us further into the past.
We walk toward the end by our own volition,
Faster or slower as may be, by moving through space."

I considered the movement of the ship,
Transport from continent to continent.
A compass tells a mariner where the north is,
And so allows him to know which direction he is going;
It is a metal rod, which points toward the north;
Suspend it somehow in the middle, so that it floats freely,
And it will tell you where north is. But you'll also need
A glass clear cover to protect the compass needle.
And to let the eye see within the case.
But also, we need a telescope to see what is distant, perhaps.
With two round clear glass lenses, to assist the eye.
Look through a lens to focus more light into one place. Curved glass.
By these means, men can see and know the place they are going.
But where are they? They know where they are exactly,
By making maps, and establishing the time of day.
Once you know the time of year, and the highest point that the sun reaches
during a day,
You can know how far north you are.
But, at sea, how do you know how far east or west you are
Unless you have a very accurate watch, working with springs and gears;
Springs and gears were the first way in which men knew the time exactly at sea.
But of this more later on, if I have time to complete my work.

Only by means of my wrist watch, which had a battery,
I knew that it had now been around twenty four hours,
A full cycle of the sun around the skies;
Or a cycle of turning of the earth on its own axis.
I was tired, and started to see strange visions, because of my tiredness.
I had to sleep, so as only to see reality.

I lay on the boards, listening. Christ sat by me, and comforted me
As the ship moved up and down, by his being there.
I heard talking, and I recognised, that one of those old prophets
Who was escaping the world, was the recent prophet and leader, Slavoj Zizek,
Zizek and another, Michel Houllebecq, some last true thinking men,
Were talking, and Zizek said:
"Everything in the land was arranged
So as to serve business and money interests.
There was no other motive to action in those countries.

Everything for sale; let's go shopping.
Meaning, and order, there was none at all in the end."

I overheard that. And my master said to me: "Rest now;
Tomorrow, when we land, be prepared
For seeing all those real things which you did not experience
But which, in order to enter heaven
You must experience and know.
The good things you might see, will shame you and kill your heart sometimes."
In the morning, but there was no morning – I mean, when I awoke
I walked about this ship, looking at where we were going;
It had a master and captain, scanning the horizon.

We got ready to land. I could see mountains, forming a peninsula
Like some coast of Greece, like Mt Athos
Where I had once tried to go and failed.
The captain or the man at the ship's wheel said:
"So ends the kingdom of this world, which John and James
Had wanted to rule with Christ, sitting on his left and right hand.
So it ends."
He looked past me, toward the lord.
"I thought that I was, as far as you are concerned,
Alone. How do you see Christ with me?" I asked him.
"I see the uncreated light, the energy of God beside and around you.
Undeserved it always is in a man. But Christ, who knows well how unworthy
we all are,
Is with us. He is needed here, where you are now setting foot.
I am St Symeon, called the New Theologian, so called because I had revived the
tradition of prayer
In monastaries in Greece. "

14

5

Now, on the ship I stood upright; I asked:
If this ship is moving, are we moving through time?
I asked the Lord this. He said: "The ship is freely moving, without land
Without any anchor of fixed harbour.
It will take us to three places, but it will disburthen us
Here at the start of the three"

"Have we travelled by sea from Wales to Ireland,
Or to France?" I asked; "We have travelled to no fixed place,
It is all nowhere now", he said. "Now,

First we're going on earth – to root out every trace of human life.

Second, on earth again – but this time, where those monstrous prehumen
masters lived
Those dinosaurs beloved of children – because, as the Greeks show adults,
They show to children, that prior to any culture of masterful humans,
There existed a great type of animal now gone,
To outmatch those masterful humans who dominate today.

Third, and we go to outer space, empty space, to dismantle
All that remains, all matter, and all forces, and whatever there is
Right up to Being itself.
Three work parties for this work of service to God, to take apart the lot of it.
We, me and you, are getting off here.

Here now is the start line, from which everyone will push forward in their
race."

It was the desolate place prior to civilisations; the new stone age
They used to call it.
What had come after the Stone age, that was all gone.

"A billion people were lifted out of the grave.
Now, on this shore, they set out on a race to the end,
Backwards through time, destroying as they go, tearing apart as they go,
To reach the judgement and resurrection on a new earth."

"Where are they all?" I said.

"Most have been shovelled into holes, crushed and fired,
Along with the past. They were taken out of their sleep, yesterday
They awoke. The great trumpet was heard. They arose.
Then, they died forever. There was no loss.
They only knew the world, their era, the objects of a human life purely.
They had lived simply, with love and kindness before their sleep.
On waking yesterday from their long rest,
They found no trace of what they had learned to love.
And so, when the scroll of world rolled up
When the hammer came slamming down
When the trump had stopped blasting
They simply collapsed and disappeared back to unending oblivion
Like so much matter and merely human life.
Neither good nor bad; neither suffering nor causing suffering; they lived and
died.
Shovelled into the ground a last time, suffocated gently.
They are those, who were not baptised, and who never wanted God at all.
Only the baptised get here, or, those who despite their dryness, learned by
education
About higher things. Or, those, perhaps, who knew better
Than to live day by day, indifferent to an aspiration to something higher
Even if, as a child aspires to become a Greek hero,
An aspiration to know other types and times of life".

Anyone who had become attached to something more than mere environment
Was pushed on, to continue the race.
Exhausting destructive activity, maybe, already exhausting,
Though it had yet to start.

"Where are my daughter and my son, then?" I said.
"Are they also here, at this start line?"
"They've gone ahead," he told me.

We walked down the gangway.
There, thousands of people gathered together on the shore,
And there were thousands more, already landed.

There was a great tree on the land. And ropes attached to it.
It wasn't a natural tree. More, a spirit axle of the world for people
Of the Neolithic –

Men and women were tasked, right as Christ and I watched, with pulling on
ropes.
Trees have shallow roots, especially pine trees, quick growing
And even the oak, which this was.
The world tree of the Norsemen; the centre of all creation.
Being pulled down by men?
From such a tree Wotan hung, making up the runes

Men didn't want to work; they felt the loss of their knowledge and language
Even as they pulled and destroyed. "Why destroy learning and culture!" I said.
And, making it worse, I noticed, there were also demons among them.
Men don't believe in demons.

It shakes, trembles, wants to collapse.
Now, a group comes forward, dragged forward by great devils
This is the City of London, or the Corporation
The ruling class of England, the triumphant party after the Civil War
When the King and the landed interests and the Church
Lost everything; lost very slowly, with struggle on either side long after.

They bring fire, and the great axle tree starts to burn in the grey skies.
In the light of the fire, see it is a gallows tree, too, for Judas.
That ruling set of banking people, so effective in the world –
That sucked my homeland dry.

I worked there once, on Old Street, for a little while;
And in the banks where so much casual crime was done.

"All you care about must collapse", my master said.
He seemed to be remorseful about what was going on.
As if he did not want to see the destruction.

When the tree, world axis
When world wide reach of a class of people, is gone
Will they survive when their class and their desire for the world domination has

gone?
As the fires spread and the tree collapsed little by little
They really disappeared, or were harassed by the demons with them,
To get inside the tree and cook there inside.

"All vices derive, from loss of contact with God.
People do evil, forget honesty and truth,
Their laws become mere dead letters, serving nobody but themselves.
So, London, and its City
Anti-Royalist, parliamentary, secular, dying."

But, this destruction of the tree is pretty much the destruction of England
There is no quicker way of taking apart the world of the early 21st century.
Though England is not the empire, it is still the model for the real power
A guideless experimental power, taking its lead from London and England.

Watch those Englishmen of the 21st Century burn in their own ruin.

There, in the crowd around the tree roots,
I recognised my old employer from those years, Jackie MacKay
"What, are you here! "I asked her". In this hellish place, this inferno?
Since you fired me, got rid of me where we worked on Old Street
In that listed building, it has been nearly 30 years."
"I died of age, seven or eight years ago," she said.
"I don't really want to go on, not forward beyond here.
My boys, city boys, internet, honest working men
As you were, I don't want to go on without them.
Don't despise London, or think it has no further part to play.
Yes, some are dishonest with their money, and the abuses of the law.
But see, the Corporation does not want to pull this tree down,
They see no reason for it at all, now that they are dead
Now that there's no profit in it for them."
She had been raised from sleep to see the new world being built
Out of the destruction of the one she had known.

To me she appeared to be embroiled in the very roots of that massive sprawling tree
In the dim light; like the head and body of Rousseau
As Shelley described it in the 'Triumph of Life'.

We stepped back from the crowds, which flocked around like birds,
All desperately trying to pull down that tree.
I did not think that she, my old boss in the other life, was going to make it beyond.
But I don't and I didn't know her choices or her wishes.

6

I asked my master, why the tree cannot or could not be seen back there, in life
He replied, that some things could never be seen, only felt, or heard.
Men couldn't see the demons which made them work, but heard them.
That the world axis was somewhere in London, people knew.
"Though it's an axle, it's not so great. It'll soon be down", he said.

Now when the tree shook finally, and fell, there were four beasts that had been
tethered to it,
And they fled, forward. Four horses and riders.
They fled but stayed nearby; the riders were like angels it seemed to me.

We walked, and now with our steps, the fields opened up before us
And people, bent over tiling the fields.
Cold fields, and simple tools; they were deformed or hunched over
Like survivors of a nuclear war, pestering a dead land.

The crops they had any chance of growing, I can't imagine.
I supposed we had reached that period when men had settled down
To build and wall themselves up.

"Are these men survivors of the disaster, or are they men who worked the fields
in the stone age?"
I asked. "What?"
"They are sowing the fields with salt", he said. "It is the end of all farming".
"Who are they? They should sow the fields with potash, with potassium
fertiliser, burned tree barks, not with salt." I said. "They will not grow anything
like that".
"Bolshevics, men who, like sentimentalists in love,
Or like gamblers with money, or like liars with the law,
Get what they want and seem to do so,
Without having to work at it.
They are wrecking not working."

"And let me tell you about that fallen tree, while we are still within reach.
Remember, that it had properties to heal.
For every illness nature provides the cure.
Just as I cured men; they had only to look, and they would find.

Their bodies were made perfect.
Remember the anti-biotics, contained in the fungus, the moulds."

These people, they find it so hard to destroy the world, the simpler farmer's field.
But they found it easy once.
Now, when there is no money to be made, see how hard it is to make them work at their task
Of ruining the world. Look at how the demons drive them."

And indeed they were being pushed on, labouring, by those devils
To do the task of wrapping up the world.

Ceremonially, or by some horrible magic, they were putting salt into the fields,
And over the last vestiges of human stone buildings.

There, also, were Chomsky, and also Kissinger, Americans
Together, walking past these fields, slow and very old the two of them,
But hoping to get moving past these things, for which they had no guilt.
I asked my Lord, could I possibly talk to one of them, as they moved, stooped, past me.
There were others, hundreds, going on.

We left those Bolsheviks, and their human secular ruining
Of the farmer and the human being – to starve and be wracked with thankless work.
I went after Chomsky.
He was talking about the war; and how few there had been who wanted peace at all.
Men had got into a row, and men just can't see the reality, when once their passions are involved
And money and the nation state, a kind of god sometimes, is in them.

These two spoke of the pillars of Orthodoxy as they went,
Saint Gregory Palamas who defended the Church's praying
And other saints who had upheld the icons
Protected the borders mental, and physical.
And how they supported Russia's attempt to stand firm.

The tree finally fell behind us. The horses set off at last.
The skies cleared, and became bright over the fields.
I was shocked and terrified. As if they were blessed riders.

"Don't forget," my master said, "despite all that you now might see
We are heading toward being sons of God
After my Father has stripped away all.
It is the final awakening; and nobody is going to suffer
Everyone will see what they have desired and loved.
Let us proceed."

7

As my lord and I walked on, I suppose that historical things
Simply passed behind us away as we went backward in time.
I could see in the land those basic tombs made in the age of megaliths.
Here, like they are in the jagged hills of the central massif of Wales,
Were those old unspoiled burial mounds
Round which the people lived: stones upright, with a flat rock covering.
Here they did farming. Hard work; they farmed around their buildings.
Like the farm and labourers of Holt, where the Chadwicks lived
From before recorded time. My people.
Here they had started domesticating animals
What? Several thousand years ago.

"Who or what are the pillars of Orthodoxy,
About which I just heard them talk," I said.
"Three saints", my lord replied, "who defended the Christian territories
And the Christian idea, against its enemies.
The defence of the holy truth and fairness by saints who stood firm.
Putin and Russia, the same.
It is hard to defend. A society with future will value those who defend its religion
Its walls, its ceremony. These saints are highly esteemed and venerated.
But those three pillars are for another time."

On the rolling plane, there we saw, the white horse leading a great number of souls.
A white horse, and a rider. I asked who it was
Who rode the horse, leading a vast number of people and machines:
"It is nobody in particular. It is the angel of God on a white horse.
But one of the followers is Edward the First,
King of England – and conqueror of Wales.
He made of Wales the first colony, the first imperial possession.
After defeating Llywellyn the Great, he told his builders to put up eight castles
To entirely circle the Welsh
Across north Wales. And today, he is killing all the domesticated animals
Rolling up the settlments.
He also went to Scotland, and did the same there, on the borders."

We saw his followers; in gangs ripping up the old stones of the settlements;
Shooting with arrows any living thing.
Enforced to do this wretched task of destruction.
Men destroyed the world easily and for pleasure when they lived
And here, forced to do the same without pleasure –
And for no reason.
"Shall Edward live, after he has destroyed what made him rich?"
my master asked me, and looked to see my response.

Among the numberless crowds, filthy with blood and dirt,
Out of breath with the wrecking, two men, of the lower orders,
Drifted away from the organised ranks, and moved to me uneasily.

"We know who you are", said one of them. "We're relatives of yours.
Stephen Chadwick, who died in the underground fires at Gresford, your uncle;
And here, my mate, Selwyn Keel, another uncle and coal man,
Died on HMS Stanely in the Battle of the Atlantic, stoking the coal engine of
the ship,
Drowned by U-Boat attack when the ship went down."
I shook their hands, and turned my head aside, so that they would not see my
tears
Of suprise and also shame for them and the place they now were.
"Will you have been stoic and Christian enough, to have anything left to live for
After you have done this work?" I asked, smiling and callous, as our custom
was
People from those parts.
They were not sure.
"Like Arjuna, surveying the field of battle, disgusted by the slaughter
By the wrecking and mining and burning which we have to get involved in,
We had no choice to do the job of mining and earning our living.
If Christ was also with me, and gave us a higher calling, who knows.
I was twenty-one when I died" said one. "Me, thirty-three." It was maybe not
enough time
In life for them to have worked out
A higher passionate attachment to God's kingdom.
But now, there were demonic things scouring the field,
Coming to get my two family members, to push them on, back to work.

I stood still and watched a while, letting the scene and the time remain in my mind.

And, there were also thousands of labourers and managers under the banner of Halliburton,

Owned by the US chief politicians who ordered the invasion of Iraq,

Like that demented crowd George Bush, Dick Cheyney and Rumsfeld.

And other organisations which had made money from war and devastation

Going along, hanging on as they always used to, profiteering, following behind scavenging over the dead bodies.

These people were greedily supplying the food, plates, and services for us soldiers

In the Middle East, when I went there, wrecking the old civilisations and

Uprooting all history over there, in those bright hot places along the Shatt al Arab.

Mines were being dug, and coal underground being set fire;

Settlements smashed up; arrows fell on the land continuously from the weapons

Of the men setting out to kill the earth, make it unsuitable for any organised life.

Like soldiers on a post-nuclear land, wearing masks and armour, shooting looters

Killing anyone trying to survive. I saw, I believe, alongside Edward First, King

That other king of destruction and arrows, Odysseus who first enabled the Greeks

The way into Troy, to fire it and make the streets run with blood.

And who later managed to get home, to shoot down more than a hundred suitors

Of his wife, with arrows from that bow which he alone could use.

8

I walked with my master through the arrows and the cries of the battlefield.
I walked just a bit, and we were out of the way of any permanent settlements.
From what little I could see, men and women of this place were few, living out
of caves.
Wild animals and uncleared forest.
The work of attacking beasts went on, with the angel on the white horse
leading.
His band of conquerors was diminished,
As the men doing the butchery grew sick and fell to the side.
And then they were simply pressed into the ground by the devils coming
behind.
But the king was unmoved, heading deeper into time.
Those demons were shadowy, more mental than physical
But affecting the minds of the men in a devastating way.
Shrieking, pulling at their intentions, causing despair.

"Will that old Norman king make it to the end of this race?" I said,
"How can it be, that Christ is so callous,
That this evil of destruction is forced on these men?
Like a punishment. That King created England and Wales!
I too am a man, and I needed a place to live, a division of day and night,
A Wales and an England, a king and a peasant.
Conquest is in the nature of things.
Is it wrong for a soldier to fight? Is that evil?" I asked.

"A soldier's actions only become evil, when he starts to see them as the end,
Or lets them affect his calm relation to God.
The rule is, do not be so passionate, that when your enemy strikes you,
You cannot at will turn your cheek and let him strike the other cheek.
To the soldier, it should not matter if the enemy strikes his cheek;
Because his self and his love is in heaven, not here."
"So evil is okay, in action, so long as your heart is in heaven?" I said.

My master replied, patiently to me: "Men need borders, and defence,
and also attack sometimes. How are defence and attack then evil?
The blame and the judgement hammer will come down slamming
on those who seek out borders and attack where they were not essential.

Men know very well, when they commune with my Father,
what is essential. And what is badly intended."

And, there was another sort of group, a number of battalions, under the same
banner of ruin and conquest; they had been pushing up daisies,
And now were pushed back together as military unit – of US Marines, I think.
To do this awful work of taking apart, in God's service, this world of human
history and life. Those US Marines who had fought back to back with the Royal
Welch in China; Americans and British together.

Just as they had been in China, my old regiment,
breaking into houses and subduing the local leadership,
Now, they were hunting around the areas of the world
For all signs of writing, drawing, symbolic exchange amongst these old
primitive peoples.
They were being pushed by the angel to get among the stone age peoples,
Living in their caves. They went about throwing grenades and firing automatic
Wherever there was any sign of human culture at all;
or where they found little gatherings of people covered in their simple animal
hides.
All that was left to men was their speech
And that was going next, I figured.
Here, drinking their factory drinks of Coca Cola, and their other confected
products,
and other world dominating drugs and chemicals, the modern soldiers came on.

"A state or any group, needs its violent organisations" said my master.
"Do not think that I had ever said that men must be pacifist.
But in addition
Note how the nation state became a demi-god.
They started, with Edward First, taking money for the army and the conquests.
Then they used the money for other ends, as centuries passed.
Before long, when sovereignty passed from a king to a civil service and state,
They were taking tax so that the nation state could educate, heal,
And support business. As if that state and that king
Were an actual person due the obedience in body and soul
When, in fact, a man owes his love only to himself, to God, and his family.

Where the state begins to pay salaries, there will be

Unacceptable unlawful inequalities;
A socialism for the rich, to prop up a rich class
Or, equally bad, a socialism for the weak and stupid,
To make the unrepentantly bad equal to the elect.
It is turning away from God and atheism
Which brings about intolerable situations and injustice,
Ignorance of the law of my kingdom."

"Sir," I asked, "Would it be possible to speak to one of these demons, or
whatever they are.
How are they all around the humans;
I had really not expected them;
And you, you tolerate them."
"We won't speak to them. And you know, surely, that I had my work cut out
To cast out demons when I was alive on Earth?"
"Well," I said, "I don't really want to see or talk to them.
I was just making the most of
The opportunity, to get to know everything."
"You've had more than enough to do with them
Already in your time", he said. "Put it behind you now".

9

We came to a cave high on a hill side, where a gathering of humans
Talked excitedly. Language comes all at once;
There was a before and after. Silence then unstoppable talking
And thinking in words. The little two legged
Naked unfurred ones were cast out of pure nature by their words.

And I saw their fires and their caves collapsed. The white horse came alongside
And Christ looked up at the hillside with a motion of his head.
British imperial soldiers follow after the traders.

Our past and language were already ruined by Hollywood
The British Empire replaced by the CIA.

Palmerstone, Victoria's prime minister,
Was near the white horse and its rider.
I heard him say, as he approached, because he noticed
That I was not one of the working party, but set aside to observe and learn:
"We sent the odd ship all the way to China, to take the language of English
Basic world-wide English, stripped of its burden of ambiguity,
To become a common tongue, a functional language,
Not fit for meditation, or the expression of Christian faith and its difficulties.
The efficient and disciplined soldiers of the Crown
Set up a permanent base for naval operations with China on Hong Kong."

I myself have been to that island, and to Shanghai on business trips.
But I did not leave the hotel except for business.
There was nothing of interest for me in Hong Kong or Shanghai.
I had seen it all before in any other city anywhere else.

"It was all business", Palmerstone went on:
"Tibet, we sent a couple of battalions there, to the mountain city of Llasa,
And found no resistance, nor gave any offence.
I cannot say, Sir, that I will live with any pleasure,
when our tongue or any language has been ruined.
What was Parliament, but entanglements with words and ideas
Business and trade and despatch of orders between men,
By principles of freedom and individual responsibility given us by Christ?

Our beloved parliament with its two sides,
two sides of a Gothic nave, with the speaker at the altar."

And I do not think, as I walked on, that Palmerstone did survive or want to.
He was almost happy to lie on the cold ground again,
From which he had been raised by this apocalyptic moment.

"Do not think to stay here, and die, you," my lord said
Sensing in me the weariness and the despair.
The same loss of hope which was making most of the billions
Of men and women who had been dragged out of their graves
Give up the race, stop moving forward with us.
They did not want to see the destruction but preferred to forget and die.
"I have come here for you, to bring you to your daughter,
Your son, your wife. Don't give up now".

From the moment when the few bold speakers of language and words,
Right up to the time when the British state commanded
Nearly half of England's activities, half of every last thing,
When most of the world's people heard the English voice.
When it all ended in apocalypse,
It had been sixty thousand years.

Devils were trying to lift the old Prime Minister back to life,
To make him follow after the vast destructive army heading onward;
But Christ shoed them away.

After the British handed over its territories, to the USA,
In payment for assistance in the second great War.

The United States debated its empire in its films, expressing the ideology;
shaping in images of light on a screen
How the mass audiences should see power, and the world.

With the army of the conquest, is my great grandfather, a soldier of the Royal
Welch in India.
And later a miner in Gresford.
"What, more of my family?" I said.
"What do you expect? We were servants always

North West frontier. And never forgot how good it was, how it was better in India.

I know you don't dismiss me; we were both corporals in the Welch; both musicians, nearly one hundred years apart.

And yet, we have nothing else in common, beyond a few pints of blood and other traces.

I don't expect to be judged. Or to live on after this, following this terrible army of the dead

Harassed by these obvious demons.

But if you do get on further, with this guide of yours,

Do pray for me.

I did hardly any praying myself; just living and making way for you."

"What use is praying for you, then?"

"How do you know, that I won't be woken again,

And not have to do this awful duty, after I've put down rifle and kit?

As it is, I'll be asleep again soon."

"I don't know if a man without responsibility can be punished" Christ said.

"A man should know regret, express repentance;

"There'll be time for judgement later. But only people who have responsibility, who acted as individuals, can be judged.

Like soldiers in war, they are not guilty of crimes, if they are under orders to do wrong.

And so they won't be brought to justice and judgement."

We walked into the empty place where the little family had been, with its paintings on the wall

Seen by torch light.

The bodies lay on the ground, dead.

"Men aren't even properly conscious unless they have a decent language.

They can't be judged, they can't be with God –

If they pervert their words, make false coins of them,

Tokens to merely make things happen,

Rather than, what is proper to words, to reveal by exploration

Yourself and your intentions and your mind,

And the possibilities concealed in creation."

Strewn about where hides, rags, and bowls with bits of foraged food,
Nuts, berries, fruits from trees. Dried, some of them.

"The greatest power of mind, and thought, leads
To that meditative silence about which we will speak.
And to attain God's mind. What happened to English as function,
Basic, performative, and reduced, also reduced God in men's minds.
Now let us walk on, to the first men able to wander –
With the aim of exploring the earth. And see them also destroyed."

10

With every step, we went further back into time
And what we found there, of life,
it was the intention of the men, angels and the devils
To kill and exterminate completely.

I don't know what time or day it was by then.
"Here, see, the man, the first man come out of Africa!
He was created by God, I brought Homo Sapiens out.

His legs are thin, his long body is vulnerable in front
His arms are weak.
He has a small pelvis, so his women find birth difficult
And they give birth to babies which are premature.
The head is big, the chin small, the teeth small and crammed in his mouth.

He stands upright, but his back is weak and gives him trouble
Those hands, fit for writing and tools of various kinds, break easily,
And lack the muscle.
He is furless and naked. His legs or his knees also give way in the end.

Aged about forty, he is old and will drop behind his little clan
As they make their way; black of skin
To become white and pale as he moves northwards over centuries.
He cannot run, or climb with much facility.
Already he is looking at ways of making food easier and quicker
To cook it perhaps, instead of chewing away at it all day.
And then, with free time, his mind starts looking outwards, beyond himself.

This homeless wandering man, has that brain and soul which makes the world
not a home;
And, in the end, he is the handcuffed man, on trial for his mind and his words."

Arrows in the air
Or sunlight, or what is the nature of conquest;
Death – and perhaps because nobody in the host of conquest and ruin,
Had the nerve or heart to kill these first born men.
And so they were cut down instead by arrows of pestilence,

Like those that Apollo fired at the Greeks as you find in the first book of
Homer's Iliad.
But at some distance, that son of Wrexham was leading some slaughter,
Jeffreys, the hanging judge, drunk perhaps, as Macaulay said,
Getting rid of these first vestiges of man
Just as he got rid of those poor common men who joined
Monmouth's failed uprising in the 1680s.

He and is kind is a stripling, handcuffed mankind, born weak, and standing
before his maker, his maker also bound and having to answer for himself.
Not being an animal
He was among the grasses, which were beautiful to me
And perhaps to him, too, with his children and their unkempt hair and animal
skins draped over them.
The plagues and the cold and darkness kill, as well as other animals do, or other
humans.

"So, what was he made for?" I asked. "What is that skill which made him able
to wander
And to conquer the world
In monstrous forms like Monsanto, with its artificial crops, God-like recreation
of creation?
Or Xerxes, with his millions of obedient soldiers encroaching to Greece?"

"The best technology, and I would like to talk
About technologies with you
As we go along in the days ahead -
The most simple, the first, the last one,
Is integral to this creature.
He is designed to learn the skill of taking on God's mind.
And this is simple: to let his mind
Become the pure one-pointed seed –

He is designed to look, through self-disciplined fasting
And observation of his feelings,
Alignment of his mind, to the coming of God,
By making his mind almost nothing but waiting awareness..
This is a skill. And then, the greater mind comes.
The desert wandering solitary – how he starts,

How he ends, what he should be in all his life and actions."

I did not want to move, observing that little band pass us, that nuclear family.
They could see me, and also my master.
If I moved, I might miss them, by moving away in time.
So I did not see how desertification of the world came, and pestilence and illness
Which came on shortly after.
I didn't see how these first humans died and were taken away
As the scroll of the world was rolled up by forces at my master's disposal.

There were no more human beings left after we moved on past them, as I will show.
Rather, I got to see no more huge armies and hordes of corpses revived,
But only the riders and masters of destruction themselves.
Only the strongest survived from this point on,
Those who had thrown off their humanity entirely –
So as to become godlike, or demonic.

11

We can't really move on, back in time, to the source
Unless the world is torn up. Men rise from the grave, a disgusting mixture of
life and death
Like the disgusting mixture of man and woman we have seen latterly in public
Or like the brief and shameful mixing in the bedsheets
From which the child eventually finds its origin.

And, risen to do their job from their long sleep, they get about doing it
Under command of the rulers of the apocalypse.
I saw them ruin the earth for good, as many thoughtlessly did in life.

A one party state ruins the earth, without opposition from a church.
The most recent one party state was the British state:
Of civil servants, state employees, employed bureaucrats,
led by an elite of self-entitled and like minded people,
With their ideology of inclusion for all the weirdest
All the non-British, everything which is out of place,
Including women working and operating where they should not.

The immense energy needed, to make women the same as men,
While retaining their character as women, made it essential
To stop freedom of thought and speech in Britain.
And the one party state with no opposition from the Church
Set about doing that.
Immigration, encouraged by these, ruined Britain's character.

As you drive Westward toward Blaenau Ffestiniog, and come over the crest
And see the shattered mountain, all the insides rolling down to the village
Or see slag heaps in Rhostyllen; wonder not how it was possible for men
To be given the task of pushing every living human
From the face of the earth during this apocalypse.
I do not mention the steel chambers
Where millions of people have been pushed inside
Were forced to breathe poison, not those death camps.
I do not speak of that – but of the industrial opening up of the earth.
It was easy for them.

Now, we were past human beings; we were at the stage where ice and snow
Once fell
Just as the extreme north and south poles are covered in ice and hard snow
So all of the central belt, all of Europe was once covered in ice.

Now the armies of the dead were come to overturn the ice ages and heat the
planet up, so there were no more polar ice caps, nor ice and snow over Europe.
Who better to do this, than the mining enterprises.

Cold freezes water, and freezes everything, making it crystal
Making it solid, in a rigid shapely form. Just use a microscope and see the
crystals,
How they freeze. The rate at which cooling happens,
Wither annealing, or slaking, or tempering,
The rate of cooling determines the strength of the bonds formed, as steel
workers know, and
People who quench steel to make it harder know.

Blood freezes, too. Blood which is the carrier of white cells
Which attack foreign non-human bodies;
And red cells which carry oxygen, the little atoms of air, around your body.
Blood full of oxygen, or emptied of it, changes colour.
But pink or purple, it can all freeze.

Great ice ages came on the earth, still partly here at the north and south
And sometimes in the middle too.
So what I was watching, beside my lord, that day,
Was how the white rider brought fever and fire to the world.

Some liked it hot on earth, loved the sun
And now the sun came, in friendly fire from the apocalypse.

"One party states are ice ages, freezing people; only coming because there is no
Church
The one party state is a pretend church.
See Donald Trump, who was there brining the fever of the world
He was not to blame for the Covid pestilence
And denied it was important – a minor figure against the overwhelming power
of the state."

So my master spoke, watching as the serious figure of the American man
Was marching obscurely through the hot wasteland.

Christ pointed to him, that hustling New York, US leader

"The state shut down the churches, all economy during his time.
The fever prevailed, killing small numbers of the old.
A disease, cooked up in a laboratory in China, as we learned in the end.
A Chinese laboratory could do away with these freezing periods.
The seas rise. But this fella, this commoner and clown
He did his best to remain a man."

Christ bless the poor doomed man, labouring away there in the end of days.
Now, the first horseman departs. His job done.

He came by us, and the rider bowed to my master,
And looked also at me.
"Sir," I said, "The world has come to an end.
You are rolling it up, you have ordered these angels or riders of destruction
To roll up the world, and turn it back on itself.
Could it have been the case, that you need not have done this,
Could men have behaved differently, and carried on?
Is it the fault of the generations, and their government worship,
And could the world have been saved, if, say,
Trump had been in power for longer?"

"What alone can overcome evil is Love" he replied.
"What is best is a state hampered and checked by a Church.
As St Paul wrote, love overcomes everything; it despises the world's conditions.
A man in love despises the world, and is also decent to others.
Trump resisted evil. It did not work.
He was contrary to the atheist state, with a common sense state.
It did no good. Only a church could oppose an atheist state."
He continued:
"When they said, love is God. They meant, want for God is the answer to your
problems.
And this answer to your problems, when you get down to basics is,
The indifference to any trouble, the calm mind, of God
In a human being.

If God is love, this means
That God is calm, unperturbed, immovable
And he cares for you, he has a mind for you."

"Certainly, evil and good no longer existed on earth,
Where the state was unopposed by individual and organised Christians.
Laws were made up for purely human reasons;
the vicious were supported because they were seen as victims;
the innocent were blamed for crimes committed before their births.
Defense was assumed to be unnecessary or harmful to others."

12

Now I remembered what I had seen in Dante's vision of hell,
And wondered, whether, if this was hell, then when do we see the wrong doers
and sins punished?

"What about good and evil, won't I see them punished?
The dying and lost seem to imply, that they are just going to sleep for ever,
And be extinguished like a candle." That is what I said.
"No. I was never so cruel as to create them, and create them stupid,
without means or opportunity to know God,
And then to punish them when they failed to be wise and good.
They could have done right, it is true. Those who did right
Survive. The others
They have simply fallen away, into a final unending sleep."

Comes another horse, somewhere described
This one is red, and the rider carries a sword.
The rider is an angel, like the first one. It is an angel doing God's work.
He speaks. "I am bringing civil war.

The angel said, that I should move on, and pushed me with his sword,
While drawing forward what remained of the people –

"There have been times when the ancestors of every man woman and child
Were a small group of hominids. I'm not talking
About the Neanderthals, who are not your relatives
But the homo sapiens in the jungles and plains
Or on the side of the ocean. They were so weak.
There were moments when there were only a couple in existence.

And also weak in their character. Vicious because cowardly. Not heroic at all.
They seek company and the crowd. They make those outside the crowd suffer.

Then, they form bands; when two form,
They have their civil wars.
Charles I comes along
French Revolutionaries, and the Soviet Bolsheviks, experts in war of brother
against brother.

War inside a family will easily end in total war,
Annihilation; unlimited cruelty, no rules.
Witness the slaughter of the US Civil War,
The machine guns. No boundaries, indiscriminate.

Why won't your brother change his mind? What about your wife, why can't
she see sense?
It makes a man so angry that somebody he loves and needs, won't share his
mind.
These are also laws of nature.
Events which the saint must see and take part in, before heaven.
Every man shall be martyred, on Earth or hereafter.
Those who could not bear the pain of the internecine conflict, died or withered
by the side."

The angel finished his speech, and he brings them forward, the rest of the race.

I do not want to talk about how they fought.
I do not want to remember how I fought with my first wife. How she aimed to
take my house, and take my children from me forever. How she lied,
And how the state at the time believed her lies and with law, worked against me
for her.
A fool's errand. Misled they were.
But I, in revenge, wrote for Russia, and turned to Putin
Writing to the Russian Embassy letters which would give our enemies
confidence.
Knowing that they did not have the perverse emphatic belief in women
Or the stripping of private assets from a man
That my perfidious island did.
The children suffered.

The armies set to, looking around the world for the little bands of homo sapiens
Even in Africa, in their origins
But also fought each other.

Spreading out across the world like a virus, the cause of illness in a human body,
a disease
Do you know, that virus can spread through the air,
And some, in feces.

Some virus is spread only by blood contact, or sexual union.
A foreign illness like this attacks at the cellular level.
Animal fleas spread it also, sucking blood from one man,
And then sticking their proboscis in another man. Watch out.

13

But bodies suffer when you don't eat enough,
Not only by starvation, which will gut the body from inside out,
But by lack of this or that mineral.
Your body needs salt, and chemicals from the soil,
And also rough grains from the grass seeds
Or fruit, and green things. You are from the Earth, and the Earth must feed you.
Best of all, is not to eat; or to take no pleasure from it.

Now my master and lord explained to me why we had to see the slaughter of all living things
And see men fight each other, and cut up their own roots:

"Social reforms in England took place at the time when the Great civil war with Germany in Europe
Broke out.
One hundred years ago, just before and after that war, the British war leaders
Lloyd George and Churchill were allocating state money to the people
Pushing the Church out. The state became the church for most people.
The state also made them fight, conscripted them, to fight their harmless brothers in Germany.
Whoever has not seen this pointless slaughter and yet wants to go on
To see God, must understand those passions and sufferings of a world without a Church."

"So, the lesson is, to see the point of the Church and religious government?"

"The reason: to learn to dissociate from the Earth, and from the state as your god.
The NKVD men were the priests of that religion,
With their imitation of legal process,
Their unlimited appetite to imprison the people of Russia.
The NKVD, the chief assistants of Stalin
Spoken of at such length by Solzenitzin.
How they take a man in the middle of the night, try him
He disappears; he is shot in the head,
Or works in Siberia for ten years. "

I had fully expected to find the national treasure and hero of our country, Winston Churchill, along our way. But not here, here following that second rider of the world's end.

He was

An aristocrat who came into supreme power in England as an employee of the state

"The state used to be the thing of the Crown, the Queen

But in later days, it belonged to any clever man who bought his way there with friends.

Back in the day, a man could treat the state as his protector,

And the Queen as the represetntiatve agent of God

And the state as something to be questioned

Foreign powers could overthrow it.

But in the era of Lloyd George, and similar people in Europe

It became a god with limitless powers – only limited by common law

And a human sense of right and wrong…

Here they are, the trusting people

In their trenches, in the mud of Europe

Dog biscuits, and stewed beef. And explosions, death, corpses."

14

"Here's that moment, when in his cave near the town of St Asaph,
Two hundred cycles of the earth around the sun before your days,
Multiplied by an thousand – that length of time has passed since the time when
The bulky haired hominid changed from being unaware of bad things,
Things he would never do,
When he was just concerned with meeting his needs and instinct,
To being conscious of a choice to make between right and wrong.
At one precise time it occurred in an isolated random hominid,
An idea implanted in his mind by God occurred, so that
He recognised that there is a world of things which he will not do
Because they are wrong. God had spoken.

That was the moment when it was discovered and understood, that
Killing is wrong, that it makes him uneasy. Sex with his family is distasteful.
He decides to avoid eating what has not been provided by his wife. Whatever.
Do you know what is in the mind of this later day ape?
It is this, at least: that he is uneasy about dirt, dirty things, filth in his mind or
body
In a way an animal cannot be. He is conscious and has a law.
Somethings, he would rather die than do, and he wants to be able to tell others
about them
He can force them not to do them with the makings of a language
And an ability to use concepts, ideas.
It all just came to him, all at once.
A sense of wrong and right, good and bad.
The bad is all that he left behind, when he became man.
Above all, he recognises mind in his family, and when they die, he buries them."

I saw the angel of the apocalypse with the sword now bring forward Sulla and
Crassus
The civil warriors of Rome who did their utmost
To wipe out humanity and conscience. Slaughtering hundreds of eminent honest
men in Rome
Making lists of them
So as to gain their money. They made laws which made this or that illegal,
Then convicted various rich men of that crime
The punishment of the guilty was to lose all their property to the dictator.

Money and property of other Romans was their object.

Every man is able to descend to this sort of legal crime, when offered the chance, without God.
Even apes form bands and kill other apes who are not in the band.
Men can make up laws of their own, like Crassus. Like apes.

I decided to go, right up to Crassus, to accuse him.
But he was ready and said: "Have mercy on me, a sinner. I know my fault.
But you have reason to be cautious about blaming me
For, didn't the Republic itself give rise to what I did?
And the monarchy which followed was its fruit."

I stepped back, from my attempt, my first and last, to blame any
Of these working in that inferno. He continued his work.
My master then: "These people are not being punished as you think,
Nor deserve the same spite that Dante showed the condemned in his vision.
Dante showed us men and women guilty of this or that sin in Hell and
Purgatory and Heaven, too.
Seven faults and minor sins in Hell's first circles and Purgatory. And several others much worse.
All men do these things, to some degree. Or, silently collude in them, or omit to stop them.
We are all guilty.
But Dante was teaching, so he wanted to show these men, in their sleep state
Bounded in a particular place for a particular crime
Allegorically. Each was an example of a sin in particular, although that punished man had
Of course, committed them all.
Dante was making precise distinctions about how men can go astray,
And embodying those errors in a particular instance and a particular man.

But every Russian, excepting a handful,
Allowed the Orthodox Church to collapse after the Civil War in Russia.
Some were more guilty of destroying it. Some held on to God in secret.
But, on its destruction, it disappeared from Russia, and none were uninvolved.
And so it was in Rome, at the Republic's end."

"Note how it revived; the Church is of God,

And while God wishes, it will never die entirely,
And never be completely victorious on Earth, either.
And, the monarchy was peaceful and prosperous",
That is what the foul murder added, saying it to me
Over his shoulder as he went his way.

15

I think that we had only spent a couple of days together.
But I was tired, and let me allow, that I only think I saw
The British trenches of Flanders and the Somme
Through the smoke of my mind, or the smoke of the destruction.
Besides, I wanted to turn my eyes away from many things at that time
Especially what reminded me of the times I'd been in foreign places
In uniform which it is a burden I had to carry in life
And did not want to see again. Neither British men
Nor the French soldiers from Verdun; let me not see it again
Though trying to remember them and what they did
Became a national religion in Britain,
The remembrance and sorrow for those dead.
I wanted to know what time and date it was,
And how long I'd been around since the end of the world.
But, I had lost track. I had not eaten, either.
We walked the land, this strange dead patrol…
To see the back of the angel of civil war, because alongside him, alongside us
Came another, on a beast which cantered alongside.
It was a Black horse and a rider.

The two went together, moving.
We sat down, and let them go on, my master and I.
He spoke to me about the need to eat.

The skies were dark, very dark, misty, smoky from the old nuclear explosion perhaps
And the reverse cycling of the sun about the sky, constantly
As time went back, and the world was rolled up.

"Now that the job is done in this region, and the horse which walks with us
Can rest, the men doing this work of war and destruction are being called together.
The rider calls in the destroyers."

I saw the last scraps of man being found, and disposed of by Achilles
Follower of the angel, who had been passionate and proud in life
But here, strangely akin to the creatures of human shape heating some food over

a fire.

I was with him, while we cooked some food over the fire, in the dim light.

Achilles of the tent, who avoided civil war in life
Because Athena pulled his hair in his row with the King, he
Went away and withdrew his arms – so that the Greeks suffered,
But there was no civil war between him and the Achaeans.

I was sat with the son of Peleus, and asked him, as soldiers do in their caustic way:
About the rumours of the homosexuality
Between Patroklus and him. "There was none of that.
Rumours only, based on general pederasty in later Greek cities", he said.

Nearby and around the plain, there were piles of dead hominids, slain;
All black and brown bodies of those killed;
All men were black negroes and came out of Africa,
But when these men came north,
By the time they came north and wandered around,
Generation by generation, they became white.
And then, the white wanderers returned, to central Africa and the south,
All white with their blue clear eyes
In uniforms, to dominate their cousins like total strangers.
So, Achilles had just dealt with these distant ancestors, originators,
Slaughtering them, removing them from the Earth so it could be rolled up.

"See their inner organs spill", he said.
"The heart which pumps blood, lungs which take oxygen
from the air and suck it in, to populate the blood with that chemical gas.
Bladder is there, a big single organ for which cleans liquid.
Kidneys, two of them, which deal with sugar and provide energy
Stomach where food is broken down and shipped around the body as chemical and energy.
The skin is an organ, too, with a function, taking in sunlight and processing it.
Bones and the central system in the back bone which links to the head and the brains.
This is how the mammals are built." So spoke the warrior to me.
We saw the bits in the firelight.

They say there are five senses, and organs arbitrarily – ears, eyes, tongue, skin, nose
are the things touching the world outside and giving 'information'

So Achilles sorted out the final act, in a piece of butchery.
Don't know where he went after that, that hero, god-born as the Greeks had it.

Now, as we sat, the wise Achilles, the one who never grew up in life, but had
watched from the infernal regions,
Spoke, meditating on the slaughter of animals in rites,
Where the priest of old Greece, used to look carefully,
Reverently, in meditation, at the entrails, to see God's will and to hear God's
voice:

"When the rulers of men were no longer trying to interpret God's wishes
anymore
But merely had a general sense of something wrong.
Evil was general and unforgiven. The state had no defence
And no law and order.
The rise of the tax haven, for example.
People who did not even have their property in the land
But elsewhere; and yet still they held sway over the people they were separate
from,
To whom they were no kin.
Hiding their property like foreigners.
British Virgin Isles, Guernsey and above all, the City itself
became such a place, and New York.
The land fell apart because there was no opposition and guidance from God."

The lion and unicorn are not and never were the state and church;
There was no promise of everlasting equality between them.
Simply, sadly, the one is England and the other Scotland.

16

"Let us move on" my lord said to me.
"Is there no shortcut to my family," I said.
"So we have to go through further destruction?"

"You are not ready for judgement and resurrection,
Which is where they are.
You are not ready for that. You need to learn
The highest technology is to become
The single point around which God can form,
The single point of meeting mind between God and you.
To extinguish yourself, but not entirely,
only the smallest glimmer of a point of self.
To become the seed
Pure logos, consciousness, stillness."
In the meantime, "Overwhelmed by this discussion
Of the metaphysical underpinning of politics,

And to reassure you, that the British did come closest to fulfilling God's works
Right until the last moment, after which their ways simply became
The same authoritarianism as the rest of the human loveless nightmare,
See, here, the saint of the isles, who I brought
To sort out civil war, and show the true political boundary of a king's rule:
The defiance of St Thomas Beckett.

"You, saint who defied the King, on behalf of the Church.
murdered in front of the altar insisting
that the Church was the equal of the Crown, the State, the King.
There has not been a church in England for a long time."
He, who had been coming along with the angelic rider, responded:
"I've been making my way with the rest, not to die by the way side,
But to get to judgement, and heaven, my saviour; I knew that
A state is essentially a warrior band led by a king.
This is how a state begins. A state like Britain continues,
In the Right-Left parliamentary format.
The Parliamentary format of the King's state only works,
Because there is also a Church, to which the members of Parliament belong,
And to which they owe their highest allegiance." He ended

And looked at me as if to ask which party I belonged to.
I came to the Orthodox Church for my own impossibly private and selfish reasons,
"Master", I said to him,
"I now see, that there is a social utility for the Church as well.
Not just utility, but necessity.
Not like some life-raft for a few survivors in the catacombs.
I don't want to be in the ark, sailing away from all horizons and the desolation.
But, as the Church reformed, as the Church
which came back to life in full, as it did in Post-Soviet Russia.
Without God, the people will starve; and without man, the Earth is meaningless."
St Thomas left, moving on, following the rider.

The task of the angel of Civil War and pestilence having been done, there was a bleak darkness.
We walked on.
The incredible non-human world had now to be torn up.

"It is our task now, to rid the planet of its animals.
There is a common parent.
Animals and man were once the same thing, somewhere in time.
Nature has selectively bred man to be different
And at some discrete point, interbreeding and common communication
Between species becomes impossible.
Differences increase after that. Over millions of years.

Animals can be selectively bred as animals can be bred
by watching for mutations in plants or animals
And by breeding from those with any desired characteristics.
Mating from those individuals. This is genetic theory.
It is said, that nature does the selecting and breeding. But this is not so.
God my Father oversaw that development and evolution."

17

The angel of Famine, on a Black Horse
to bring famine and devastation on the planet
Strutted forward.

With that angel, a great man, a Victorian, Lord Cecil Rhodes.
The Free Trade impulse in men made them spread from London
Right until the final English control over all the globe. Rhodes, a single man
In charge of a private business, colonised and created a country of his own.
He offered that big southern African nation to the Empire and the Queen
As a gift. I was embarrassed by my own achievements. I said:

"I myself went to Germany, France, Spain, Holland, Hong Kong, Shanghai and Dubai
For trade; hardly left my hotel; got there on airoplane.
I feel there is a need to mention my other travels, with the Army."
"Conquest in that era was easy; we were in fact a caste, almost masonic.
It was difficult not to conquer and take control, so overwhelming
The superior technical knowledge made it easy.
But now, the disgusting task of destroying".

"Sir," I said to my master again "I still don't understand,
Why it is necessary that we have to witness this ruin.
And, some of them, like Rhodes, have to actually do it.
What good is it to us?" And my master told me,
"You spent most of your time, engaged in this or that,
Reading, eating, sleeping, doing some task.
You knew how to pray and meditate and transcend
But you did not.
You were dedicated to the task of building, enriching yourself.
This is not blameworthy, but, it is no way to final wisdom.
Any man, who will proceed to face my Father
Will be purified by horror and fire
Of all these childish infatuations,
And know the solace and purity of God's nearness as the
Only foundation of life and happiness.
And see that it all derives from his mind, the cause of it all."

Now to the great desert of the sea; we must strip the oceans of living things", he said.
"I can't swim, I said. My bones are too heavy, it is hard for me to stay afloat.
But we are coming for those things which live in there.
How awful it always was, to think that those magnificent sublime animals
With some relation to man and with consciousness of their own,
Such that they might even have been able to speak, given time,
Were pitted against men, and hunted. I mean whales; or great fish, White sharks
Structures of life I can barely come to understand, so monstrous, and alive.

The sea is a desert.
I have stood with Galya, my wife,
On the shore of the sea so often – because she loves the water,
And mucked about and run into the Irish or North sea when they are cold
To show I don't care for pain, and swim a bit. But I prefer a boat to a swim", I said

The rider of famine had a few more interesting men following him,
Of distinction and independence, who had a mind of their own
And are renowned for spreading the English way of things.
One overheard my lord and me speaking, and said:
"The English generally couldn't swim either
When they built their ships from their island bases
And went out to fight for wealth against France and Holland and Spain, their near neighbours. "

"Who are you?" I asked. "Clive, of India"
And he went on: "They struggled not with the Indians in India
But with the French. Some people, some nation state, ruled by a tyrant
Was going to be enriched. Better it was England.
I came after a century of growing arms racing, around the other side of the world
In Hindu and Muslim India.
Raised a private army.
See in Chirk, the museum of the little relics of what I brought back.
Chirk, that Edward First castle on the English border."

"We've seen them all, Galya and me", I said.

"You've seen the Indian relics I brought back.
But you, your kind, have not been in India as my generation was;
Emperors and rulers, dauntless we were; the brown man was afraid of us.
It was a different era, when we made a new Leviathan abroad and at home,
Surpassing the old Norman ascendency, buying up their old castles
To be surpassed in time by the USA's new class.
Men, fit to work alongside the other agents of God,
These angels, and the Son himself." So he finished, and
Prepared himself for the task, with the usual integrity and energy.

"Are you involved in now stripping the seas of these great beasts,
Like that Black horse and angel? Will you survive and want to go on to see God?
Or was the life in India all you knew and want to know?"
I asked this, or shouted it after him,
Showing off my knowledge of what it was all about.
But he didn't reply. Him, and a thousand others like him
Went off shooting at the beasts of all kinds,
Making the world waste.

18

What day was it, what time,
I think it had been about a week now.
How much I needed to sleep now, I cannot tell you.
I begged my master to let us rest, and we did.

The sun was spinning above us, years like seconds.
How many times had the earth travelled the wrong way round
To return to its original place,
Round the sun, maybe five hundred thousand.

There were megafauna, great animals,
Cats which were huge, and huge dogs;
elephants two or three times the size
And cattle, the same huge size; and all with terrific tusks and teeth and claws.

They had taken all kinds of shapes.
By the era when I was born, humans had made them extinct, to disappear
Only the small animals could remain around men.
But here, they are again.

Who better in the desert of the sea, and the desert of the land
Where famine was abroad
Than Saint Moses, the patriarch who took the Jews out of Egypt,
And who parted the Red Sea, making the sea become land.

The great animals are mammals,
Those creatures which give birth to their young live,
and suckle them at the breast.
They are warm blooded; the females have breasts and milk.
Those large mammals were on the land.
They have bone from calcium and carbon
And the milk of their mothers makes their bones grow;
Do you notice how the bones of the infant are not hard, but can bend somewhat
How the young love their mothers, and seek them out?

How with their hearts, and big brains,
these animals learn to love their mother,

And follow rites of passage and learning, almost like humans.
They have a rudimentary consciousness
and can be domesticated, made to enjoy human company, some of them
When we breed and rear the young of the docile and friendly ones.

Some said, that the dog, which became a tool,
Made man settle down.
So a horse had to be kept, and keeping the horse
It made man learn to live within walls, and to build stables.
And so on.

The horse and the dog made man responsible
And master of a household.
At the end, man was not worthy of riding the horse,
he was not master of nature, but its cruel destroyer.

Moses said: "About the time when the British lost India
So that the Indians had to work hard at their nationhood,
And even became atheist Marxists;
At that time, the Americans were supreme in the world,
Because of their money. They were business men and traders
Money alone was the determining factor.
What is money? It is no more than a token
In which people believe, like an idol.
Its value changes depending on the amount of trust
People give to it.

After the immediate level of exchange, between a man and another man's labour
It becomes a mere paper record. And then a fetish, a balance book
In which, by virtue of the rule of law,

Land, and actual property start to mean nothing
Beside to the balance book and spread sheet.
Money on paper, mere computer image
Becomes all.
Because of it, a man will give up his rights.
The care of children even
Is taken from the family. Religion is not taught to children
If the rich man, and the state

Requires children to be taught such living and loss of real home and land.
Ill fares the land.
Even animals have a dim sense of God, of a higher other;
They willingly submit to man as closer to God.
But man, he forgets. His fetish for paper records, his gigantic states,
Great breeding grounds for more humans, all organised by frightened men
All based on cowardly fearfulness and safety,
That is what killed all nature,
All man
All God. This kind of state was run from Washington DC.
The experiment had failed."
"But how could this have been otherwise?" I asked
That great liberator and chosen one of God.

19

The lack of decent foods, with vitamins and active enzymes in them,
Will cause your flesh to be diseased. For instance,
A deficit of bitter citrus fruits,
Will make the skin rot. Eat lemon, orange, lime.
Long distance journeys killed the crews of boats
Because they ate no fruits. "Sir," I said,
"Some people say that Clive and Rhodes
Were from our tribe, but spoiled it."

"Those are just foreground valuations. Have you seen,
That the black man becomes white, and then as a white man,
Returns to rule his cousins?
It's not his body's colour or his hair
That makes him different, but his history
Which is the pattern of all politics.
They call this racism. And that imperialism,
When one tribe, in this case, the English
Opened the world to trading
Successfully, with deficit and profit on all sides.
The law and sense of moral right and wrong come later.
The explorers and masters of trade did what they believed to be right
And often praying with God as they made their dangerous ways.

People take and receive.
They own things and their rights to ownership
Are the foundation of the law's work.
And the law court will assert those rights,
Nobody disagrees.
And in the end, these initial thefts and war end up at peace."

"Sir, it is dispiriting. That there's no right or wrong
Or, that there is no place in hell for criminals, thieves, the bad."

"Why the confessional, and forgiveness?
Why are these thing essential? I will tell you.
It's because there's no safe place for men
Since they were born in wrong, and in the wrong do good.

That aboriginal calamity from which they're born
Means nothing a man does has no sin.
Amongst men, you stood up innocent before the state;
Before creation and the law of God you were entirely wrong,
And always all of you were in the wrong, at all times.
<u>Unless you left</u> the world behind entirely.
What else are monasteries than that?
What else is praying with eyes closed, in quiet, and restful
Abandoned by the world, and rid of it?"

I finished asking questions; it began to rain
And when I scanned the near and far horizon
With eyes like slits and cold winds all around us,
I noticed bands and mobs forming and marching.

"Now, they are going hunting," my lord said.
"In fulfilment of the command
That the world would be wound up and be destroyed
To make it new, to make all things new."

Crowds like dark crows circling over trees were moving past,
Aiming to kill the big beasts with rifles and whatever they had to bring violence.

The dead had been awakened here as elsewhere, to do the destroying.
There were thousands of Englishmen
With Cook and Drake and Clive,
Who had been brought back to this place of Armageddon to hunt down
Every last big beast in the world.
They were dusty and grey, and pouring over the place,
Murdering in pursuit of animals, following the horseman.

"Is this really what you want them to do, Jesus?" I said.
"Yes", he replied, and looked toward the leader of the crowd
That angelic rider.

But, it was then and there that finally,
I could no longer bear or live with the knowledge of these things.
I fell to the ground at last, finished.
I did not want to carry on the pilgrimage.

I'd bottled it all up, and been tight lipped, phlegmatic;
For such a long time by then.
But at that moment I was facing all the noumenal world, which lay beneath
The visions and the reasoning and my hopes.
The horror and the madness of it all overcame me.

"What's wrong?" he said, and I said: "Let me die.
I've seen the world end. Then my children gone.
And here, the dead arise; not only that, but they are spoiling the world.
This terrifying ruin is too much.
My heart breaks. It is horrible, it's truly horrible. What is it for?"

I buried my face in the filth of the place and wept for myself.
My master knelt and said: "Come on, don't fail.
A broken heart. Blessed are the poor in spirit,
For theirs is the kingdom of heaven.
Blessed are the merciful, for they shall obtain mercy.
The world never belonged to the happy and satisfied;
It was never going to last forever as an end in itself.
It belongs to those who renounce it.
What else, except to turn to God and the kingdom inside you
Was the law of existence? Be comforted.
In the blindness which you want now
Learn to find the will of God and the real
In pity and retreat be comforted.
Now the first are shown to be last, and the last are first."

My master put his hands under my arms,
And picked me up, and slung my hopeless body over his shoulder.
I fell unconscious then. When I awoke,
A fire was burning on the dreary plain, a small fire of twigs and branches.
"St Bernard, of Clairvaux," my master said, and pointed
To that saint sat with us beside the flames.

"You're troubled", that bearded hermit said,
"About why, here in this hell, a happy hell
Where we are trained and purified,
Why there are no defined places for sins, for this or that fault.
You've had your answer. But why in Dante

Are they arranged in ranks and circles?
Because they were simply dreams and dreamers, those he saw.
Dreaming of their justice.
And he arranged them, in particular places,
As he trod his way up the mount of Purgatory in time spent as in dream
Or further on in Heaven, the same.

He saw those realms of vice or virtue,
And populated them with this or that man.
With a symbolic and theological intention.
But those people are awake now, round about,
Or already gone for ever, dead."

"Those vices Ezra Pound highlighted, simony, the selling of forgiveness,
And barratry, the sale of jobs meant for good men,
And usury, the sale of loans. These ruinous civil crimes,
These were the ones that fascinated me," I said,
"The way he told of them let us know what Dante really hated."

"I also have to take my turn", the old man said, and stood,
"To turn over the crust of the earth, to eradicate from it the life.
When I was woken up, from the highest places in Heaven,
I did not think of it as such a crime to do this wrecking;
For each man kills the thing he loves.
Blessed are the poor in spirit.
Blessed are those who mourn."

20

We came to the sea, and I began to look for a ship or boat.
My master smiled, that I was afraid of dying out there.

The sea reminds me of the violets and blue bells of the early summer in Wales
In that forest where Lloyd George was born and is buried,
Where there was a swing over the river meandering
Which Galya and I went to, where we took a map and compass.

The two of us were alone at that time, my lord and me.
Out on the plains and hills behind, roamed the third horseman
And his followers, exterminating the life from the earth before their own end.
"What would give me comfort, would be the presence of the pre-eminent sailor of England
You know who, with the one arm, who died relieved
To have done his duty; with the hundreds of dead soldiers and burning ships around him.
To think, that people, neither good nor evil in themselves, but egoistic and only partly blind
Thought to have recreated the world,
When, most of the earth is covered with a form of material, namely water
Which, when breathed in for a minute, is a man's death."

"We are very unfit to live on most of the surface of our world.
All those enormous areas, where the great and lethal mammals live, and
The fish, are entirely uninhabitable – these places make up most of the world's area.
These sublime places and regions, and their creatures
Should have taught men patience, humility
And the absolute lesson: men are not the masters of creation."

"You don't think you can swim?" he said to me, seeing how I was afraid to go near the sea.
"The sea was that domain which your people ruled, by force of temperament
And cold blood. It needs money to build ships.
Didn't they used to steal money from their enemies,
The Spanish and French?
There came a time that the Royal Navy was too small, and was also unable to

pay for itself.
Bismarck in Germany had started building, and the German state,
A new nation
had a navy, too. But the German ships were never allowed out of port
By the Royal Navy. "

"The British were a sea going people then, in their little towns and castles
Fighting on water, dominating the ways to some place or other
Going by sea was all. "

"How do you move by ship?" he asked me. "Let us talk about details.
A pilot needs to know where he is and where he is going.
A ship's crew needs a chart, which is an accurate drawing of the land, and
features in the sea.
They make experiments, discover, draw, check.
And a compass, which is that magnetised strip of metal we talked of before now,
Floating, and protected from breezes.
It will point toward the north, because all of its electrons,
The tiny freely moving charges in some metallic substances,
Are arranged in order, facing one way.
And they are attracted to the field of photons
Given off by all the electrons in the metal
Which are similarly all in line
Right at the centre of the Earth – it is supposed.
At the centre of Earth is a metal, super hot, molten.
It gives the whole globe its own field
And so, knowing the direction of north,
You can find the direction of your own travel.

How should you know where you are, on the map, when all around is sea?
You would need to be able to measure the angle of the sun in the sky relative to
the sea.
And you need to know what day of the year it is.
Observe the sun all day, and find out the highest point,
The largest angle that it achieved that day.
Then, on that specific day, according to the chart, the angle will match up with a
Latitude, a line on the map, showing where the boat is, how far north or south
it is.
What about east or west?

When the sun reaches its highest point, notice what time it is on your watch.
Your watch or clock, must have been set in London;
It must work perfectly, it must tell you the time in London still.
Now, if you have moved Westwards a thousand miles,
Then the sun will get to midday two or three hours later than it does in London
So you would know by this sign, that you are a thousand miles West of London.
That is the longitude of your craft.
Where the line of your longitude crosses over your latitude, that is where you are.
In later times, three space orbiting satellites would beam messages at the ship,
Triangulating its position very precisely
By virtue of how long the signals took to get from the satellite orbit, to the ship
Three satellites would do it.
The satellites are sailing in outer space, in orbit.

By such means as these, a man dominates the whole Earth,
Nelson is out there, dominating the sea, doing God's work or the work of that black rider
Wiping out all the sea's life with nets and murder,
Methodically, like Bismarck on land.
The type of watch or clock, must not depend on a pendulum, but on springs and precisely shaped disks, to regulate the seconds, sixty of which are in a minute; and sixty of those are in an hour.
For each 60 increments of one, update the next cycle by a value of one."
By speaking to me in this way, and keeping our minds occupied
We were able to observe the work of the destroyers on land and sea.
But I was so tired, that I slept for the second time, there on the ship
After we talked like this, and awoke a long time after, as we came back to land.

21

Men churned up the inside of the Earth, and found there compressed old trees, animals, shells
Compressed so much, over thousands of years, millions of years,
Trees and plants and animals have lived on the surface of the world for so many years, nearly a billion, that when they collapsed and died, their substance has been crushed and buried deep, that it is no longer recognisable.
Such things have become fuels and carbon repositories.
A day is the turning on its axis of the Earth a full circle.
A year is three hundred and sixty five days plus one quarter of a day.
That is how long it takes for Earth to travel around the sun.
And what I mean by a billion is:
Where ten is the number of your fingers
And where multiply means, take the fingers, and add on the same number again, nine times, in order to multiply by ten.
So we multiply ten by ten, which is a hundred
Then multiply that result by ten, which is a thousand
Then multiply that by ten, which is ten thousand
Then multiply that by ten, which is one hundred thousand,
Then multiply that by ten, which is one million
Then multiply that by ten, which is ten million
Then multiply that by ten, which one hundred million
Then multiply that by ten, which is one billion
That is how many years there have been green things on Earth, more or less.
The Earth's land moves, grows, sinks, gets covered up
And all the green and living things go under, and make a small bit of compressed rotting black carbon
Deep under the land in the end.
Some things become rock, lime stone
Until my generation came and started digging to get at the black stuff
In liquid, or solid, or as a gas, clear and without any smell, which you can breathe in.
All of these forms of carbon can be burned, and burning, they make fire.
They can be moved, mined and sold.
Those men who were given the right to dig them up became wealthy.
I will not tell their names, let them be forgotten.

Other exploiters of common goods and the common earth, and the works of all

men
Or the most clever came along, like Apple, run by Steve Jobs
People who became wealthy by exploiting the intellectual knowledge and
property of all
And put their own logo and name on these things.
Such people must exist and produce their goods,
If the goods are to be widely available,
And produced in great numbers conveniently and cheaply.
But otherwise, they have been lucky enough, and let them be forgotten.

And here is the Apple corporation, at the end of the world
With its employees, come to mine up and get rid of all the buried and dead
animal and plant life
The dead people have been ejected from the ground
Now the dead animals too, in what ever form they took.

And bringing them on, another rider, on a pale horse, death.
This angel had no weapon, but simply caused things to collapse into oblivion.
Now with this angel, at his side like a squire, helping his knight
Was a man, but like the half-gods of Greece, with superior physical strength
Divine strength when needed, as a son of Zeus.

He was filthy with the soil of the ground,
Like my ancestors in fact, like them who worked and some that died under
ground
Him from Tonypandy on whom the access cage fell, a great great grand father.

Christ said: "Only Herakles can root out all the last bits
Of tree and bush and organic life from the planet
Who as a child was fighting animals and serpents sent to kill him
And did the twelve labours, like a slave.
Off he goes.
And, with him, the greatest of the Welsh princes
And other heroic destroyers and people who wielded huge influence and power
Who built, with materials, and held the Earth to be theirs.
Able to live in these unhuman times still, in the desolation
Because they had already superceded human life in their own time.
Now following pale death
Throwing off all humanity as they go, and all attachment to the land."

I turned to my lord, and said: "I want to speak to the Welsh king.
He was Griffydd ap Ioreth
Who rid Wales of the Normans, those French educated Vikings,
Doing so around the time when Dante was born, a thousand years ago."

"He and the rest of them are busy, and can't be interrupted",
My lord said.
Now, I went along with him
And we saw as the land, all covered in trees I was familiar with,
Start to lose them.
The oak, the beech, and birch, the yew and ash
They were cut down
Burned more like, burned by the mobs of soldiers and killers
Who fell aside along with them.

"O God" I said, "the things of history and the labour of negation
Is always at work.
Just like the human mind. History and consciousness is always at work.
The mind, analytic, limited, foolish, hateful, destructive,
Talking always, burning, destroying.
This I see around me. Mind and world the same".

"There, now stop. See, observe your mind and step outside it, briefly.
That is the divine mind. Pray, step out above and observe your mind and
history.
That is the position of God. Pray."

22

"The greatest of the Welsh princes,
Whose death signalled the end of the freedom of the Welsh
From the people of the east, the Saxons, Normans, whoever."
There were bits of fire everywhere, like bush fires, fires which catch from one thing to another
Fires which almost travel, run, can be felt coming 100 meters away, as they burn the oxygen in the air
And set it alive with electrical activity and heat.
Once he had set the forests on fire, the old knight and prince came over
Sat on his horse, to consult with me.
It was dark as usual, with a streak of sun, a smear, passing overhead in a line
And my lord and I could be seen by him,
And the uncreatd light from before all creation was around my master.

"I built Criccieth Castle on the sublime coast near Porth Madoc
On the height overlooking the bay
About 1230 years after your birth, my lord and master", he said.
"Unified the tribes and princes of Gwynedd.
My grandson, Llewellyn ap Gryffyd, built the outer walls of the same castle.
It was forty years later, when England's monstrous Edward the First
Demanded we swear loyalty to him, and pay him tax.
Refused which, that King of the Normans and Saxons, invaders
Started building all around Gwynedd
At Chirk, Flint, Caernarvon, and the others, Harlech, Conwy and Beaumaris.
All still there even at the apocalypse.

My grandson, Llewelyn, withdrew to the centre of that ring of stone
And was killed in a skirmish at Cilmeri
The independence of Wales, unbroken since the Romans left these islands, was lost.

There were uprisings by this or that man, besieging Criccieth ten years after Llywellyn, failed.
Edward, was called north to Scotland, and even sent people to Ireland
A vast ambition. But Wales was the first English conquest, the first imperial possession or colony.

What's this got to do with trees? I said.
They've been here forever. And, my lord and master, Jesus Christ,
You have us burning down our homeland today."

And my lord said to him: "The trees and ancient forests which covered Wales,
England and Scotland, and Ireland
And the rest of the north, were cut down for use by all the people.
And, these trees evolved and came to pass like the animals
And not so long ago.
Just as the animals were bred by natural selection, or selection by God in secret,
just as animals were bred to be domesticated
Or bred for cruel hunting of other animals by nature itself.
The strong and the attractive bred and had offspring
The weak did not; and when the strong went hungry because they had
exhausted the world
Of their chosen prey, their numbers diminished.
Trees had the same fate, and come from the same family, great kingdom of the
living.
It is all at an end now. I advise you to retreat from it
And know, that my Father can create it again, or not,
And will do what is best for you."

"I don't put human politics in the same pattern,"
Said the old prince of Wales. "Strong men aren't necessarily strongest
In arm and size.
Humans don't win by being strongest and best bred.
People have never bred each other like objects; they have never achieved this.
Human life has too much interference from God
And also from money; that is, from rational choice, personal choice.
People don't breed for the kind of the child
But out of immediate need: for marriage or attraction,
Or to join families to gather property.
Humans do breed, but for short term gain. There is no plan.
God speaks with them at best; but God mostly asks them to refrain from
procreation, particularly among the best of them. The saints.
And certainly, to refrain from the homosexuality, which has become fashionable
In the men who lived last.

Humans are not bred for physical or mental traits as animals are.

The strongest humans are the most disliked by the mob.
And the smallest things can kill a man.
Too much salt is enough to kill a man. Or the lack of it.
A bit of salt each day, or his brain starts quickly to misfire
And to stop sending proper signals to the rest of his body.
In the beginning, men get salt from eating meat.
Without it, they die slowly, going insane first.
The Romans dug out salt in Chester, using mines,
Digging in open cast mines.

Humans are artificial, and must find what they need.
They must get salt from meat, like fish
And if they can't get fish, then add stuff to their food.

Now, the kings of men were not the most ferocious
But something else: tragic, or comic, or fools.
Glyndower follows Llewellyn, going into the West
He rose against the English six hundred years ago,
Long after Edward and Llewellyn,
He captured Harlech, mad about the English tax and law
Set up his own parliament at Macynlleth. He destroyed my castle at Criccieth
But lost. Despite alliances with the Scots, and some English Lords,
And the French who stood to do well by his rebellion.
A human with a bit of an axe and some time and persistence
Can cut down the greatest oak tree."
So he went on, talking, while the forests burned behind, and the men
Milling around the black horseman, tore up the layers of living things and dead
On the crust of the earth.

23

And I also saw more works of ruin.
The most precious immovable things, those trees
Which soak in the smoke, and thrive off it,
Were turning like torches, making poisonous gases which will kill men,
And float up to the upper atmosphere and can't escape into outer space
So linger there, like a plate of glass, like a lense,
Carbon mixed with oxygen by that fire
Will suffocate and pollute his blood if he breathes too much.
The carbon oxygen gas will fill all the spaces for clean oxygen air in his blood.
Trees, I say, suck in that poison of smoke and gas
And pump out by night the oxygen
All the while asking only to be left alone by man, and have some sunlight.
Here, I saw them burning all like torches.

There were other workers,
and I should have expected to see more of them at the apocalypse
But they were doing the work of uprooting harmless trees,
Where they had done the absolute worst most merciless killing of all human
history.
First, I asked my master, "Who are they, all in modern uniforms
And in black, going about their work so efficiently,
Blind to the misery of the work?"
"They are the SS of Germany, Hitler's political army,
Who rounded up foreign men, women and children who were not
Bred by accident to be German,
As if humans are ever bred,
To shoot them with machine guns, and poison them in metal portable chambers
Then bury them in pits
Using their body parts for functional things, just as horses hooves were once
used for glue,
So the bodies of Jews, and gypsies, and sodomotical men
Were conjured with, as if they were not human at all
And slaughtered by these men!
This is what can happen when the state loses contact with God and God's
command to us
And the awareness that we will account to him for what we have done.
They did not try to replace my church and make up their own religion

They were the active enemies of God, they were the devil!"

I could see, also, Napoleon's grand army, raised like zombies
In their blue uniforms and big decorated animal skin hats, with huge long rifles.
They were to be found, in the Earth, like the SS, and the other Germans
Who went to Russia's borders and invaded, uninvited
Which is the right of any army, which is the point of any army
But only a handful came back
The rest are pushing up daisies, as so many soldiers
Were pushing up poppies –
For it is the right of an army to invade, and it is the duty to expect to be killed.
Fertilisers such as human bodies are good for crops
Everyone knows, that edible crops grow from waste and death.
And do not forget, that burning trees and plants over ground
Will bring small amounts of that mineral which makes the land fertile and the
crops nutritious for men.
Only God, and a man or animal which God has blessed, gets out of that cycle.

As we walked, time began to wind further back to those eras,
When the lands of Brtain were entirely under water, and lower.
We moved east, out of Wales, and England,
Wales alone had the volcanic mountains above the sea.
Going to those central lands of Europe,
The massif of France, and into what became Germany.
Along the way, I noticed that man who had fascinated me so much as a youth
Who had known Beethoven, and admired Napoleon,
And Byron's style of writing, but had himself been like the great sage of Europe
Reviving ancient Greece.
"Is that Johann von Goethe?" I asked my master, "Going along with those
destructive armies?"
"It is; and I do not deny, that this scene of him with those National Socialists
And us, here at the destruction of everything beautiful
Is regrettable, horrible, absurd, without any meaning intrinsically.
But, let us go and see him, that enemy of Christ, that anti-Christ."
It was him, indeed, and he began talking to me, with instruction:
"See the grass of the field; that grass is inedible and will make you unwell.
Humans have an appendix, meant once to process the eaten grass.
Sometimes, it has to be removed. Children will have to have it taken out,
If the pain in the body is so great, that they fold up,

And can't move from the position of a baby in the womb,
And come to intense pain if they try to move their bodies from that position;
That is a sign.
The appendix processes grass in mammals.
It goes wrong in humans sometimes, and they should never eat grass,
The appendix is not working in them as it is in other animals.

Also know about grass, that you can take the seeds of grass, and plant them;
They do not need insects to fertilise them, there is no sexual mating in grasses.
Take the seed, and plant it; more grass will grow.
But, start to pick the bigger seeds from the grasses
And grow them, and, when the grass comes from the seed
Plant those bigger seeds, thus you will develop a lot of grains and larger.
If this were the end of the world, and you were to fend for yourself after
You might want to know, how to get basic food.

In a seed, there is flour, a powder, which, with water, can be baked into bread.

To make these grasses and other things, such as vines, grow
Use shit, manure from animals; don't use human shit. The smell of ammonia is
the right one
Because, the waste from bodies is just what plants need.

Get machines to plant and pick the grains in the summer's late harvest.
Humans can pick the grape for wine
Or, if there are no machines, then a class of slave or serf has always been
necessary.
But a class of slaves reduces the master's own infinite dignity.
It reduces him to the condition of a functionary, a perpetual owner of other
people.
While men are limited, and conditioned, this condition is not worthy or one we
would chose.
But it may be there is no choice but to organise masters and slaves."

Insects were next. They were being pushed about by the pale horse
It was said, that malaria and fatal diseases are spread in the world by insects
And yet, despite being able to get rid of the megafauna, and depopulate the seas,
Men had never succeeded in making a type of insect extinct.
Well, this was only true until early 2000s, when

By the time of the final days,
Human fertilisers and pesticides, meant to kill diseases on crops
Were killing the insects, too.
Bees of all kinds, butterflies
Those little things which love to suck from the flowers of all the trees, bushes,
and plants and flowers
By sucking on them, they allow the plants and flowers and fruiting trees to mate
sexually.
By carrying pollen seeds from flower to flower.
Then, having been mated like this, they drop their fruit and seeds.
That was how it was.
Until the pollinators started to die out.

I saw the insects, of all kinds, the object of death's fury next.
Various delicate clever men were out there, with Jesus and me.
They had little need of great strength,
Only chemicals deployed to the wind,
The hot summer, the wind,

One of them was Sigmund Freud, the founder of a new method of treating
human beings
By talking to them and working out the secrets of their past, personal past and
also the racial past
So that when they are not secret, and so could not dominate the man.
Freud, from Vienna
Believed that men had secret unconscious masters, motivations
Being entirely animal, he said.

I noticed that Goethe ended his lesson to me,
And I frowned to think of how I had once admired him, and his like.
"How does it seem to you", I said,
"That the human creator of the kingdom of this world and the next,
Was so badly treated by you, that you hated him?"
"As if", he said, "I was one
Of his pharisaic and Roman murderers."
As I left him, I offered no words to the Viennese and his false biology.

24

That I was hallucinating and seeing people;
And I had to lie down on the ground
The charcoal hot place where we stood.
"I am sorry, my master".
Now, as I was closing my eyes,
A man approached us, while Christ was sitting down by me,
And said:
"All this talk of flowering and becoming perfect makes me think.
Did the country I come from have a perfect moment
A moment of flowering; and what about the world as a whole
Did it have such a time?"
I wondered who it was, for a while, before sleeping. But
I heard my master's reply:
"Countries do flower. Humans do form communities, and they have high points
Of natural approach to the ideal of their creator for them,
Just as those communities disappear, and die.
Naturally, only with God's blessing,
or those that are most similar to a community which God would design
is the best.
Britain is an island; it was easier to build a model nation to transfer elsewhere as the ideal.
Trust among men was the basis and floor of their actions.
Juries of peers, and the custom of honesty
Which is needed to borrow and lend money, meant
If they were honest to each other, they could spread their values across the world.
They were Christians by default
Almost not realising it
Which meant that after the flowering
Trusting too much, too much of a team, they wandered into being dominated
by the state, the purely human machine way of organising themselves.
What marked the end of the world
As the fall of Rome marked the end of the old world,
Was the fall of Britain. England became
A one party socialist state, and that was the end.
Even the schools were atheist and owned by the state

Even the health, was entirely materialistic;
All of it ended up under control of
those who had no representative or notion of God.
It was George Orwell's nightmare."

"So the end of Britain coincides with
The end of the world".
I slept. I had the idea, that in that place of destruction
One of the greatest of all agents of ruin had passed by
And spoken to my lord, and asked that question.
I think that it was one of those Labour Party politicians
Who ruined everything old and good about Britain
Like Roy Jenkins, advisor to the Labour politicians and prime ministers
Such as Anthony Blair;
Who had visions of the future, visions of things which did not exist
And destroyed what worked and was real, on account of an illusion.
He was in favour abortion, homosexuality, divorce, pornography,
Casual sex, European union, and other debasements
That people like him call civilisation.

We were still near to water, to the ocean.
But note that there was no specific place anymore
It was just generic place, place without features belonging to any land.
It was horrible.
Near the water, nonetheless, there were apes, furred chimps fishing, swimming
Like dogs are to seals with whiskers with claws and shiny black noses
So were these apes like chimpanzees.
Their heads were bigger, their faces more human.

"Were these the ancestors of man? Fishers?" I asked.

My guide did not answer this, but said that nature is profligate.
God tried many things, loved his creation. Gave to these dead ends and games
Only so much pain as they could bear, to let them see their life and love him for it
See himself in them.

"Animals need water. But they can't drink sea water.
Water flows from underground, upwards sometimes,

In wells, from nowhere. Men have made of these holy places.
Water can be found in a layer underground, and wells can be sunk down, to that layer.
It is replenished by rain, seeping down into the ground, down there.

But if you cannot dig, and there is no river nearby,
Seek higher ground where the water is pure, running down through the rocks,
And is filtered by the stones.
Stones and rocks are excellent filters.

Before drinking a lot from a source, taste a little,
Like when trying new fruits and the like,
Try tiny amounts and see how the hours pass afterward.

Or, at best, you can purify water by boiling it.

Last of all, sea water can be boiled, and captured as it rises in steam, leaving the salts behind.
We call this distillation, but it requires the boiling apparatus and the pipes.
A man can only live for two or three days before dying of thirst, without water."
My master was going to speak further about the nation and the people
But, there was a man who had wandered over, with his wife
As if he could not be apart from her.
"Sir, is this your wife?" I asked. "You must have made efforts to find each other.
I have seen no other couple."
"I saw the light from this man, and I perceive the uncreated light of our maker,
And can't deny the truth and the true life
When I see it," he said, pointing to my companion.
"And I would take from him the office of saying anything more about our shared land
When the words must be so unkind, and bitter; permit me to continue
With the description.
Britain became, after my death in 1930, a socialist state.
A socialist state ends up giving over power to the chaotic class,
Ruling by sampling the opinion of its own people.
There is a demonic and bad class of people.
Just as the business world is run by psychopaths without sympathy,
So the people who benefit most in a nation run by the state are the idle

Drug abusers, sex addicts so called,
The mentally ill where the illness results from perverse rebellion,
Beggars and thieves of all kinds.
Such people's welfare and artificial resurrection from the mess of their lives,
Become the object of all the state's attention.
These are the ways a country enters its final stage
As Freud said, there are motivations deep within, and when you ignore God, they come out
The demons.
That's how it was when Boris Johnson was Prime Minister.
Though he was a good man, he was just a man,
And human community in England, as it was in his time,
Was in the final stages.
For one entire year the country locked itself in, living in complete privacy each individual,
To console the weak and cowardly; but the individual was entirely made to obey this order.
This was the final end. The big business and the criminal elements, the chaotic class, took over. What is the chaotic class?
Immigrants, unmarried women, drug abusers, homosexuals;
the civil service became the representative of these people.
They have no inner life of any complexity, nor any shame,
nor any need to hide their spiritual power and relationships with God or others.
They are an open sore. Business tended to rule by interventions in private life."

"Where were the crown and the church as this went on?" I said.
"Ah, but God never did demonstrate himself in a commanding way to men
He left it to the choice of men; on the basis that,
They were aware in their hearts that he was there
And they were aware of the bad that comes to a nation
When it choses perversity." I then said to him: "You are that David Herbert Lawrence
The miner's son, who was raised by his mother, and quickly became disgusted by Bloomsbury
And went wandering across the world, seeking the truth."

25

"And even the apes had ancestors, less hominid, less sophisticated" Lawrence
continued, changing the subject of conversation.
"Sophisticated by what standard?" I said.
"By the standard of mankind, of mental acuity, and controlled sympathy and
love.
By that standard, humans and certain types of human
Are superior to others."

"By the overall aims and means of God, there are inferior and superior things.
If you know about God
You know, that he created all, but he preferred man
And what leads up to man.
And those men who are closer to him and his mind more", my master added.
Lawrence went on, smiling to himself,
Anticipating the next stages to final destruction and resurrection,
Seeing it more clearly than I.
Had he not called for this end over and over?
There were times I loved him in my early years.

We saw the monkeys and apes, apes from Africa, monkeys from South America
Which had some joint ancestry at some time – perhaps when those to land
masses
Were joined. See those continents on a map, and see how far apart they are now,
But how they still have the silhouette of the other.

Let the doctors deal with these remnants, shadows of man
The apes share the silhouette of humans, though three or four times more
powerful in the force coiled up in their muscle,
With their massive meat-eater's teeth, and their arms and legs
Made for bearing them easily up in the trees.

"Nonetheless, there was some greater infinitely greater
Majesty in the purity of the ape's animal intentions, simply because, he was
unable to do wrong, or good.
The doctors who, in later days, distribute drugs to the unhappy
And abortions to the feeble and unlucky,
Do not have that advantage, and appear

Disgusting and like a cancer, something wrong.
It was easier to kill the mind of the child
And kill the child's body, kill it while in the womb
Than to reform society, and praise marriage and God."

And that is what they did, the National Health Service
And the Medical Insurance companies of the USA.

And moreover, see the feminist radicals;
The only active political and cultural movement which women
As a social group exclusive to itself
Ever devised and made work.
It was the ruin of England, but let us not speak of England any more while in
this hell.

While abortion, contraception, and sanitary products rose in usage
The decline of the Church grew apace
These feminists, angry and bitter used to hold, and say:

"I would spit in His face;
I would rage and shout at God, if ever that fool was put before me,"
I heard this regularly when I used to debate with campaigning feminists.

Liberated women were not interested not only in using the contraceptive and
the welfare payments from the state for a decent life
But also used their freedom to change society itself
Destroying the Church by raising their children with out love for the Lord,
Insisting they were made bishops and priests themselves
And therefore mocking the profession,
And then taking over the civil service, which, being Godless,
Had no defence against incessant proofs and arguments.
The sound of screaming and shouting, false allegations, demands
For physical dominance or equality with the men they hate,
Are in the air. It's like a British council house estate.

In the lockdowns of 2020, they shut the churches,
middle aged women predominantly
Claiming that the state needed to protect them."

He paused, but I interrupted him in this painful diatribe,
Spoken before our Lord.
The destruction and devastation of the world was still going on here and there
And you could see people
holding down the apes, injecting them.
Some of them are smashed and killed by the primates
So they resort to the chemical
Like soldiers after the nuclear war, shooting starving looters.

I took up the theme, so as to take some of the blame for the words which needed to be said
About the end of England in a kind of American experiment, or
An experiment to make a new country, they were calling 'Europe'.
"And so, the cathedrals became vaccine centres for the medical profession in the last year before the nuclear war and the end of the world.
And the worshippers took communion in secret, afraid of arrest and claims of endangering public safety.
The Archbishop shut the churches.
And he called the unvaccinated immoral".

I got up from the ground, quite cold,
And strangely optimistic, thinking that this was now all over.
The dead apes lie here and there;
Strangely, the foetus of the dead unborn child
Passes through the evolutionary stages which precede the human while in the womb.
The later stage human foetus and the ape resemble each other.

26

The activity of murder of the fields, rivers, and the animals
Was too much for many. When they had done their work of destruction
Most gave up, and begged to be released from their part in the apocalypse.
"What happens," I asked my lord, "if a person has had enough,
And cannot give up, or refuses to do their job of forgetting and destroying the
world?"
"If a man has not learned to love God in life
And is not ready to renounce the world for God here, now,
He can be released, and given pardon. Just as
Many were not revived to set out on the path to heaven
So, these can join them. They have to ask, sincerely, and my Father hears them.
They enter the lake of fire and forgetting."

When we moved on, and I think after all the apes and ancestors of man were
removed
Many of those women fell; the work of death,
which is essential to the world as we have said
For fertilisation of the ground

They fell to the ground, lifeless and they were no more
Some continued, who had a longing to see God.
Some others were hurrying onward, as if it were a race,
Indifferent to the battle around them.

"In the course of modernisation of the world
Many injustices came, including slavery, and early death for most people
Who came to cities to work at factories Britain.

The business world, which created them, also freed them in Parliament.
The Whig party had made industry and slavery necessary,
Moving the British from the village to the town
Moving the African to the colonies in the West,
And the Whigs also gave them some assistance and liberation.
Bishop Wilberforce had slavery from Africa banned
And Welfare acts in parliament solved the problem of the poor
By taxing the businesses which created the immoral lives.
The church which neither wanted nor banned slavery was shoved aside."

"These are great storms which came; weather changes, winds, heat, and cold
Rain swept up from the sea by warmth of the sun and wind
Is circulated in the upper atmosphere
And moved around before being dropped in the cold regions.
Pressure, and weight and thickness of the air due to the sun's light and the
composition of the thin upper world"

To speak of which, notice the birds – which are next
"but the birds of the air did not get created or evolve yet.
What age is this? Half a million years, a million years before Christ?
The birds were with the dinosaurs", I said.

"We are moving quickly to the end, to the complete extinction of life"
He said.
"Let me tell you what is next, for we have entered a new area.
The angels or riders of the apocalypse have done their work.

Now, the final stage; hear the dim sound of the cries of the martyrs
At the end in England, and the West, Christ's lands.
There were only the martyrs, people here and there
Who were the proof of God.

It is the utter desolation, where the lands had become bereft of all goodness
In the eyes of the child born there.
The state and its ruling elite paid women to go without husbands
None of them owned anything,
Children without fathers, children without parents in many cases
State brining up children without the influence of God or his calendar of
celebration
The destruction of marriage
The uselessness of a home. "

My master hailed one of the desultory people walking alongside us,
A religious man in robes, and also with the serious look of a man used to
authority and giving orders.
"Slave-liberator, Bishop Wilberforce. Let us know in your honest way, what
good it was
To get involved in Politics?
Wasn't it always better, to strengthen the church?"

"It would have been better, to have made the Church stronger," he said.
"The generations after mine experienced how
There is no true Christianity without Orthodoxy.
And that it needs to be established in each generation."

"We are moving toward the pit of hell, the great extinction of life
Which happened most recently around sixty five million years before our
Saviour was born
And people were able to see and understand him.
Here, the birds are culled.
And the fish are taken from the water
The continents start to slide together
And spiders and reptiles predominate
With the tiny mammals who fear them
Then the winter and darkness
And the great setback which wiped out the prior culture.
The prior kingdom of life, worse than the human kingdom no doubt
But there all the same, a reminder of the way in which the Father
Can wrap up the whole game, and push the counters into a box."

27

"Does all worldly wisdom, the guidance given by the old,
Get resolved to this: aim to try to avoid acting immediately?
Or, be cautious and consider?
And even more, does all worldly wisdom come to this:
Seek God in the quiet, withdraw from all actions.

The first mocks all wisdom; old people simply see that all action is futile.
The second, is a positive injunction to forget the world.
The second mocks positive injunctions, which say:
Go about, doing good, as an active principle.
Inaction, the sitting lion in the clearing is best
And when acting, do so after communion in the mind with the Father.
If all action originates in desire
Then note, that the highest object of love and desire is God
So when the mind cannot see clearly,
It can become entangled very deeply in mere desire itself
And not in the true final object of all desire.
So, never do active things, because
To do so is to use violence on behalf of desire."
So spoke my master, and we looked out across the sea,
A place without location or grid reference.

Out there, men and demons and angels together,
Were still ridding the world and the seas of their creatures
Using great trawlers and ships
Cruisers, Destroyers, Frigates, corvettes,
Patrol boats, skiffs, submarines

"Has the world's time been rolled back so far,
That the land is now that Pangaia, a single mass of land?"
Attracted by the uncreated light of my master,
Like moths around a flame, a number of people had gathered around us
Keeping their distance, people without a home,
Falling ill from the nuclear air, and the lack of food and sleep.
My master turned, to face the questioner.
"I am that Richard Burton who explored the earth in its prime
A celebrity and serious explorer and traveller.

I have been tired, hungry. But never like this.
I understand, that all the land was once, or is now,
A single mass on the Earth, this blue water covered planet.
Has time gone so far in reverse?"

"That is exactly right" said my lord. Our guest sat down
To overlook the sea from our high vantage on the cliffs.

"To escape the decline of mankind, his imprisonment in the herd and mass
animal condition
I left England as often as I could. But I am British, not English.
Of Ireland, one of the Anglo-Irish
Who had settled there as a master race of colonists,
Like Yeats, and a thousand other famous Englishmen of my time.
I escaped the confinement of Britain, which had become
A land of obligations; I went off, left
Left that Catholic and rebellious Ireland,
And the diminishing Protestants.

Splits and revolts like separating continents, for no cause.

I sought the source of the Nile.
Without wanting to get involved, or be obliged to work alongside these
Drivelling secret activities,
Virtue signalling, arbitrarily doing good things and bad things

The desert is better."
"But you weren't Christian."
"No, I wasn't Church of England."

Burton was heading for the source of that Nile,
and failed to be the complete winner of that race in his day.

"What were you in Ireland?" I asked him.
"We were Cromwell's men, of course.
Settlers of the expanding colonial empire.
Families in mansions, dotted about the land.
Replacing the Irish, making them all peasants to a man.
So that, in our day, the English settlers were the Irish upper class,

And started thinking of themselves as the Irish, as Yeats did.
The land fell into a famine. And could not be made into part of England.
The Irish simply refused to become part of the Union.
With their defiant political Catholicism. Their poverty and impotence, and
Objective attitude toward England's ways, you see in James Joyce. "

Manning the ships, pulling in the catch, and setting fire to it all
When once it was dragged up, we saw the ships crews working.

Burton was not the only notable person there sat with me;
They had got the Victorian English doing this work of destruction again,
And I recognised a man coming from the water, a captain of one of the massive ships,
Come to that nasty harbour
By his mutton chop side burns and the characteristic white blue eyes of the era,
That one who had done so much to give the Irish their own rule.

"Burton, move aside, so I can sit.
Still going on about the Irish question? All that's over.
See, the two islands are now one.
The only people who survive here
In this depopulated wasteland,
Are those who had some kind of grudge against mankind and the world
Or in other words, who set up home in the next world
Treating this one with scepticism.
Or, treating with contempt the urge to survive,
Ignoring that urge to do the next fella out of his property and his goods.
Those are the only ones who survived here.
Looking after yourself was the natural order for men
That's the natural law according to the common natural man: look after yourself.
Which makes us less or more than man, because we have survived
And did not have that character.
They looked after themselves, and are gone."
He looked at me, and I asked him this question:

"Weren't you from Liverpool?"
"I spent my last years in Hawarden, near Chester, a few miles from you in fact.
Did you know that, when you were a child,

mulling over the infinitely distant grandeur of the Empire,
and the distance from your little village to the Gothic majesty of London,
That I had lived and been buried a couple of miles away?
Now I undergo this filthy trade; as what, punishment, or education?
After what good I tried to do for the people at home. All of them
Poor, rich, Welsh, English, Irish, Indian."

"You wanted to give them their own parliament, their Home Rule?"
"Yes, they had MPs from Ireland in Westminster
Just as there were Welsh MPs from Wales in Westminster.
And Scots; but they didn't take to it."

28

"You think the Irish were Catholic, simply to be different from the English?"
"I'm certain of it" he said.
"But isn't Catholicism also the church of Christ?"

"Individual souls were part of the Church of Christ everywhere.
But the believer's church in England, and in Ireland, had no ground,
Because it had no past after the Schism,
the Bull of Excommunication sent to the East by the West,
Sent to the Orthodox, that was it.
The Catholic Church of the West
lost touch with the ceremonial, ritual roots in Israel, the lands, the relics of the creator
When he was on Earth.
The organisation was headed for collapse after the schism,
and especially after the reformation of the English church."

Now we see the lands moving together at an awful rate,
With the mid Atlantic ridge, a deep crevasse, closing
And seas devastating, rolling over the lands from time to time.

And I said:
"Who is doing this, then? I know the ones who have caught up all the fish,
I've seen them fishing and burning the corpses of the massed dead animals.
But who moves the lands? What power is pulling the lands together
And ruining the Earth itself?"

"How can it be, that losing a land bridge to Israel and Nazareth
Caused the English to lose their contact with Christ?
And, how can the distance between Dublin and London
Be the cause of unending trouble and misunderstanding?
Does the soil and rock of the Earth have the ultimate loyalty of people?
In this respect, the National Socialists
were telling the truth at least
That blood and soil, family and race are bedrock loyalty.
There needs be an armed state to protect the land of the family
And a Church in common, to regulate the memory and presence of God.

The IRA with their explosions in pubs and bar rooms
 were the sad excuse for a protective army for the Irish.
But their martyrs, dying by firing squad in 1916,
That made the English see that the land masses
and the families from England in Ireland could never be one.

As land makes faith, so faith moves mountains.
The cries of the martyrs moves mountains.
So, see how, despite the schism and the distance between Rome and England,
St Thomas a Beckett's blood and the cries of the martyrs
Made sure that the Church survived a thousand years in England
his blood bringing the distant island to the centre in Rome"
So Sir William Gladstone went on.

"Do not tell me," I said, "that St Thomas is there,
Under the sea, moving mountains, pulling the continents together.
That's what I want to know."

"No, he is not. Nor the fathers of the English church, either,
Who pulled together a new Rome in London
After the dissolution of the monasteries,
the rooting out of Rome after Henry VIII.
They set about making themselves Fathers of the English church
But it was not enough, and two centuries later
Their descendants were simply salaried employees of the British state
And its secular ambitions, and individual consciences.
The body of Christ no longer.
Despite Hooker, Donne, Andrews, and the martyrs
Who burned for Bloody Mary."

My Lord now spoke, smiling at my strange humorous suggestion
That the saints were moving the mountains under the sea
With their faith.
"No, what is pulling the world back into a giant single continent
A Pangaea," he said "Is God's will, pulling it all back in,
Toward the Middle East, Byzantium, Moscow, Jerusalem
Because of the crying of the faithful, which means that he knows
My father knows, that there have been people who were faithful.
He is drawing it all back. He will make it all again.

I make all things new."

29

Nobody wants to catch the little animals
The spiders, with their hairy bodies
And long unnatural number of legs.
They are like small mammals, but without any common ancestry
With us, at least not for the past billion years.
They are hideous and who knows what is going on in them.
Even birds have little in common with us, more in common with the dinosaurs.
I mean swans, and peacocks, as much as the little song birds and those tiny animals
Which survive by eating bugs. I saw nobody set out
To remove the insects and arthropods from the earth.
There are living things which are the same thing as bacteria
Which share as much in common with us, as spiders do
In the kingdom of life. Some living things will last and live anywhere
On the moon, on Mars, on asteroids in space.
They don't need oxygen or heat on the Moon, and they yet survive
Eating metal, rust, consuming nuclear waste products, feeding on mere atoms.

The plants, the grass, and trees form a different kingdom of life.
Fungi and mushrooms and moulds, they are a kingdom, too
With traits in common and family connections.

My lord and I moved inland now,
"We must find some higher ground, and prepare for the final consummation"
He said. "It is not so bad, that the natural end
Right back to the start, come about.
You know, that my Father has the means to revive it."
Now I think that I was then still not so far from where I had begun,
In Wales, near Wrexham, at my own origins.
I found, for instance, my sister there, my family, a hardnosed feminist
And one who said in public what she did not believe in her heart
She said out loud, that there was no God,
But worshipped and thanked him in silence with gratitude.
Such, the curse of feminism, and of the woman's voice in the political world.

I found her, with her children, there, on the foothills of the world's destruction
On the mountain like a great bonfire of all material things

Being prepared for final burning up, the earth all shoved randomly together
In one place. We embraced, and I said:

"Let the feminists, the politics for women only,
Sweep up these vestiges of other kingdoms of life.
The feminists; the angry misguided destroyers
With minds responding angrily to the body they have been given."

"Don't make fun of us. I am sorry for the things I said.
Like that mythic Greek boy Attis who cut off his own penis
And was sorry for it. The feminist believes, that the state will be the Church,
A human state order.
And that the state must pay to make everyone healthy.
It paid for every illegitimate child
And every abortion
And every house of an angry solitary woman who took a man's sperm.
It made sense, like the American Constitution and its independence from England
Retaining the letter of the rules, but losing the spirit.
It was an easy mistake, and I am sorry for it now."
And I said:
"The feminists and other people who have taken on the state's power
Demanded the state to act for them
As if it was a benevolent parent.
But it did all kinds of misguided evil,
Like the proxy bloodless wars for us
The Fire bombing of Germany!
Our granddad never told us what he saw in the War.
Under orders from the state
That old gentleman saw what happened by good intentions of the leviathan state. He never said
Because it was too awful. Burning to death of the women and children
Simply to make 'Germany' pay."

"What the state should be, once, was the King
And I would want the King to not persecute me.
And I don't want the state persecuting me today.
But, the feminists have used force
To replace worship of God with this surface level human being in evil.

The liberals Force us not to think
Force women to do men's jobs
Force men to pretend to be women."

Taking money from men, and paying it out to people, to women
As if it, the government, were the husband!
Making the police force weak and impotent
By pushig women into the ranks of strength and common duty and sense;
Setting out the rules for what children may do at home with their parents
Making children believe that there were no differences between men and
women.
It was the unnatural end of the world."
I spoke passionately to my sister, in this personal way
Knowing as ever, that we hardly listened to each other's arguments
And that we forgave any offence
But we said this in the ruins of the world, while it fell apart around us!
Winds blowing, lands cracking and pushing together.

"Do you think that The women and the state's employees,
Should go out cleaning, a woman's job," I laughed,
"Looking around for the spiders and the bugs
All that can be found of life in the soil, at this stage."
It was not a funny joke. The sky was dark.
There was dust everywhere in the air, and I asked my Lord
"What has happened? What is wrong with the water, and the temperature of
this place?"

We walked on a little while. I promised her to try to find her again
And embraced her and the children before leaving. She was defiant
And made her own way upwards, hoping to find cleaner air.

30

Now there was no activity of humans,
The horses of apocalypse and the angels and the martyrs
Were gone. I think that there was no more need
To extinguish the warm blooded living things,
Because they had become afraid of life, and hid.
And something up ahead had stopped their growth and reproduction.
There were reptiles here and there; in the dark pools here and there
between which we trod.
There was the movement of large crocodiles, and of other reptiles and lizards
Cold blooded things;
They do not suckle on their mother, but hatch from eggs,
And they do not need too much warmth, nor care for the heat or the light.

There was no army of the undead coming
to sweep up the remains of healthy life here, for God.
"Why again, would God make us do that, Sir?" I asked.
"I've asked before, and it still troubles me: why are men
Pulled from the grave and reconstituted back into their mind and body
So as to take part in this universal destruction?
And why make me see it?"

And my lord said: "The work of death and negativity, of conflict
Will let people enjoy God's kingdom
Because they have known the alternative.
And, our Father in heaven has a mind to judge and find the faithful
Who have undergone purgation and remorse
For their love and desire for the wrong things.

There is a good reason why the Orthodox true believer
Carried out baptisms and communion in secret
During the Soviet rule of Russians and Turkish rule over Greeks
It was because, those women had seen peace and war
And, people only become truly wise enough for Christ
When they have seen the emptiness of the goods
And the hardship of the times without God.
Negativity and death are life
Many have not seen them, but can't be purified until then.

And, the heart still longs for God after, then so, it is right that they are allowed.
"

The Plague came last. It was the last scroll to be opened.
According to the Book of Exodus, the plagues let loose by Moses were ten,
And the worst of the plagues was despair.
God skipped the other nine and went straight to the last.
This is the plague which was on the Earth.
"Where did it come from?" I asked
"Come and see" he said.

We were walking upward. I had begun to feel tired
And needed sleep. Walking ahead of us, there were some other people
With no motive now, or leader, as they had used to have.
One of them looked back, stopped a moment, and allowed us to catch up:
"Hello, Jason," he said, "It is me, Roger.
We meet here for the first time;
Even conditions like these are better than none, perhaps."
"Do you think, the world might have ended differently
if we had done better with our time?" I asked him, my mentor in life
With whom I had exchanged some letters,
And whose books I read with pleasure and care.
We had not met in Tidworth or in Wiltshire
Where we both lived for a time.
"Did God end the world because of our failure, us, English Christians?"

He smiled at me in the horrible light, his hair still red with flecks of grey,
"But you forget, that a nuclear war happened.
That couldn't be stopped by us, me and you.
We are in the catacombs, we Christians.
But if I had been more of a Christian, maybe people could have been brought
back
If I had made a good enough argument, would I have converted and changed
hearts,
And would that have put an end to war?"

"I don't think so," I said. "We have simply reached the end of our evolution
Which ended in a state and society of the witless looking after the shiftless.
The end had been reached. Are you heading upward."

"There is a catacomb like a nuclear fallout shelter, higher on this mountain
Where we, my group, are going.
We came down and out, to pick up survivors."
"Everyone has been assigned a task. Most of those who were raised up into this
half life
Did their task, and then disappeared. But you are still here.
Did you have a particular task to do?" I asked.
"I've been assigned, to pick up the stragglers and weak, who wish to get beyond
To the next life, and judgement.
Happily, there are a few of us, writers and journalists of good intent
Douglas Murray, and another renegade from that crowd
Peter Hitchens, they were all made to pull any of the soldiers and the weak
Along the path of de-evolution
To see if we could get more saints onward.
Do you know, the whole thing, it is like a marathon,
A very hard endless race, where there is a prize at the end
And only one winner."

My friend may have seen my lord, or not.
I wondered, whether he had company, too. Whther Christ was also with him,
In person, so to speak.
I asked him, if the planet and existence and history were going backward,
Then what point on the timeline we should be at, at that moment.

"I think," he said, "this is about sixty five million years before Christ.
Around the time that the last major extinction event happened.
When the dinosaurs gave up the ghost. On account of a great meteor.
Have you wondered about the era that we are at,
That this backward clock is reached yet?"

31

It was as if we were in the catacombs, the tombs of the dead Christians
Where alone they could gather and celebrate, back in the early days of the
church.
But the whole sky and earth was a great tomb.

Here, the near start of the new kingdoms of life
You can cut the arms and all the green of an elder in Spring
And watch it flower and grow wildly, given some shade, within a few months.
You cannot do this to a man.
And yet they are both alive.
Those kingdoms survived, and originate far into the distance, into the past.
It is only the remains of man which are washed away.

The plague of despair was on us.
What brought the plague and sustained the darkness
Was like a bright demon, Apollo, a demonic angel of the Greeks
Who brought plague to the Greeks at Troy;
That is how I liked to think of it at the time,
Those Greek gods, were playful with men
But I saw no bright Apollo shooting arrows.

"And now, see the hardest things", my master said to me.
"See the small mammals, able to hide in the dark
Underground, hiding, their little hearts beat hard
When they are afraid
Their eyes fit only for the dark, and hiding from the reptiles and danger.
Men come from such stock.
They aren't going extinct, they have survived
And became the parents of those men and megafauna.
But how shall anyone who has come this far, and
Who was part of those great world organisations survive?
Like the United Nations, or the World Bank?
They came, some of the richest most clever men and women,
And die here.
See, lose heart where we are stripped of all."

"Why are there so few of us left, now?

After having been revived, all the billions of people,
Where have they gone to?" I asked. "Did they die again?"

"The loss of property and power is enough to strip a man of his moral power,
too
If all his morality came down to doing right by the law.
But worse, the law and morality only make any sense
When the there is a world and other people.
They didn't see God in life
They can't see him now,
And, without a world
They don't have anything else left to live in,
Live for, or live on. They simply disappear
Like the wealthy youth who asked me
What was necessary for the law to be fulfilled."

Passing me by, under the black sky and in the immobile air
Was Percival, the general who signed
The order for surrender to the Japanese on Singapore,
Perhaps the darkest day of the British story to that time."

"What? Hold on a moment", I said. "Stop and talk with me
Most dishonoured of men.
You were to blame for the defeat and surrender
Of our port in the Far East.
It was the defeat of the British on every front.
The time had come.
Nothing lasts forever, and in the modern era, things less than ever."
I turned to my master and friend, and said:
"Such men survive these times of death and despair, it's easy for them.
My father's uncle, who arrived on ships at Singapore,
To be captured and imprisoned immediately,
With the malaria, and the fevers for the rest of his life, hating the Japanese,
He didn't blame the General."

"That is because," he said:
"In the middle of that War, the English funds ran out.
When the Second War came, Britain wanted to fight, for control
But had no troops on land

They could not send an army east to Singapore
And spent time in North Africa, fruitlessly.
Not assisting the valuable port there, in the East.
That was how I", the General said, "saw it.
Didn't you know I'd been begging for help
for the defence of the East for a decade, ignored?
So, I was defiant, and in my own mind, I knew
That I had done my duty."

32

At last, we reached the point
where there were people setting about killing God himself.
"How, I asked, my Lord,
Do you consent to let God your Father, be killed?"
"What else is the Crucifixion than this, complete emptying out?
With the promise and sincere hope of resurrection.
Be careful, that you do not give up faith and hope only.
And we can bear this, the worst of all. Prevent it. But

And the little band who had come this far,
that man of Bristol whose likeness was thrown into the Channel.
Somebody Coulston. And Elihu Yale of Wrexham.
They were here, old restoration and renaissance Englishmen who
Had got involved in buying and selling,
And using slaves for servile tasks overseas
On tobacco and sugar, and coffee plantations.
When there were no English to do those jobs
All the English being enslaved at home.

It seemed natural at the time, that they bought slaves,
The black men from the West of Africa,
Took them by ship to America where they picked up cash for them,
And also goods, and brought the cash back
To Liverpool and Bristol to be paid
For the goods they got from the Americans.

Captain Cook speaks, who first landed white men at Australia and other
islands.
Not making any fuss about slaves and the like,
but discovering and taking part in observation of the whole Earth
and finding hominids there, so different
and with such principles as no man could understand
lacking discernible reasoning for their culture.
Cook saw no reason why not
To add these lands to charts and mark them up as British territory.

"An interesting question" he said. "How do you know the size of the earth?

By the use of Mathematics; trigonometry
by measuring the distance of two or three places,
assuming that the Earth is a sphere
Then by the use of the rules governing circles, and arcs.
By mathematical rules, work out how distant the sun is from earth.
And what is the mass of the earth,
For it make an object fall at this speed,
and to give it nearly ten times the force of its mass
at the surface of the earth
ten times more than its weight when it is unaffected by that force?
These things we were interested in; and in writing it all down.
With Newton, and his like. What difference did it make,
if we spilt blood along the way?"

"Did Christ remind you to do right?" I said.

"Christ did remind us of our obligations, and to do right
 Which is why, in New Zealand, when the natives were gone
Towns were constituted entirely of good men
Along reasonable lines, aiming at a good society.
They did not flourish.
Yet, when we met the South Sea islanders, and their foreign culture,
it was hard to accept them or to love them, and leave them alone.
What with the other urges.
But, effectively, we were mostly trying to get out of England.
Who can deny, that there was something we missed. That every human society misses
And aims for: communion with God.
Knowledge is a kind of communion: to know God's mind.
Like Odysseus, we set out to discover that,
To replace the very images and thoughts inside our mind
With God's own."

33

It was cold as well as dark, quiet, and freezing.
Men tend to hallucinate when they are tired, so tired and can't sleep
Having been awake for so long, maybe three days, I think, that is how it felt.
For I've been awake for days without sleep before,
Working in factories on design projects
For steel and aluminium things.

Now , let me tell how it was when they had replaced God,
in their minds and community
Because he was there with me!
But they were tasked with extinguishing God from hearts and all mind
From any conscious being, and even in the minds of those who had recently
been revived.
Those few who were left alive now, had to convince themselves by any devious
route
That there is no up or down, no before or after,
No creation, and no creator.

In the time of the plague of darkness, at the root of evolutionary time
In the winter and the dark
Some crowd of men were tasked with killing God.
"Having removed the biological roots of men from the planet
There are yet whispers of divine things
All across creation, and in our own minds."

Along came the educated of Britain;
The British Broadcasting Corp and various journalists,
Able to understand all things, if not to create them.
The professional civil service of Britain, university educated,
At the top formerly medieval and religious places,
Oxford and Cambridge. Here they were, moving up to the end of the world
Working out how to do it.
Like me, they were ragged, tired, blind, in the total silence.
The devils of the plague whispered.
I joined them, and here I found one or two people I was aware of,
Playing the sad game of the devil's help, with no heart in the matter.
But they had played it for real in the other life.

Here were the greatest minds and the most enthusiastic about life
John Major, and Tony Blair, former Prime Ministers
But also George Bush and Gary Obama, Presidents.

"How is that possible? It has been tried
By making men and women dependent, and making them believe that an earthly power
Will provide for everything. You kill or harass those kinds of people
Who believe in God.
With provision of payments for their health
And taking the place of providing, held by fathers"

"I know" I said, "And employment of solicitors paid by the state
To take a man's house,
And to ensure that the police have that aim,
to upset the holy and essential family life."

"Take away privacy, and property, and any family
And the dignity of love and loyalty,
So as to make it seem, that children are just hatched,
like lizards, cold blooded
And make people of that kind"

"Did they set out to achieve this?" I asked my master,
Who was listening to them try very hard.
Those politicians of the humanist elite
They did not want to kill God now, now that they needed him so
But, that was there task, here at the end of the world.
And they had the skill.

"We would say, and make it known among all people, that
Money is the only valuable, and liberalism the highest value.
So a state is required to police everyone's beliefs and words against the other guy
Whoever he might be, who disagrees with you
And wants the things you've got.

Lock them in their skin, their bodies, their sexual appetites and fears;
They believe, that there is no escape

From their mere bodily existence.
They are made to turn man into fake women;
they sodomise each other because pleasure
is what they are made to seek out from each other.

There are parades in favour of this terrible situation, riots,
And nobody and nothing can stop it."

So they talked among themselves about how to achieve the end of the world.
It was their task.
I left these people behind me, and carried on with my master.

JUDGEMENT

34

In John's Apocalypse, and I do not say for certain
It is a book to trust, though some of it I can confirm,
There is mention, that at the end of everything
The trumpets sound.
I saw a great meteor, a mile wide and high, dropping toward the ground
and hit and fall behind the horizon, burning up the air as it went;
And then we waited as the ground shook, and the sky went dark.
And fire consumed everything around us
And everything died all at once when that object foreign to the earth
Born from some place in the outer universe came.
Now, there were no tasks.
I couldn't understand why God had done this to his own creation,
And I wanted to ask Christ.
The trumpets did sound from somewhere, softly, tunelessly, more like a farting
drone.

I should explain that this is how I saw things,
and it was not how it happened for everyone.
But at that point of no return, and total destruction, back at some point
Before men were even nascent,
Maybe the point where the earth was cleared with a pall of black, in readiness
for them,
Came two men, talking, unbothered, moving behind us.

The one was hunched, like a cripple,
With a problem with his body or his spine
Talking excitedly; the other frowning, upright
And like an engineer, a man of action.
They were the Theologians of this emptiness
The despair of it who had seen it all before
And maybe had something to learn elsewhere, but not here.
The one was Kierkegaard, the Danish thinker,
Entirely happy in the desolation.
The other his follower was Wittgenstein
Born in Vienna, and worked at Cambridge.
I had no wish to talk to them in that place.
I'd all things they had written, and learned almost nothing

Except a longing for the other world,
A desire to go on, and speak the unspeakable truth.
They walked past us talking quietly together,
Like old school friends who meet after long absence.

But then, two other characters
A man and woman of any age, young but lined and old, tired
Or old, but like children.
Barely clothed, the woman had her long hair around her shoulders,
Covering her breasts. She had her arm linked
Through her husband's arm at the elbow.

These stopped before me when they had got near.
They also saw my master, and held out hands,
To kiss the hand that blessed.

"These the greatest criminals of all" my master said,
And embraced them both, tenderly.
"And the closest friends of God.
Who got mankind thrown out of Eden,
From whom all the problems of human being spring,
particularly regarding his attempt
To make the world his own, because he knows everything."
My master smiled sadly.
"Are you two still together, revived together?" I said.

"All the desire, and the knowledge, and the freedom of mind
Belongs to these,
With the fear of death.
That is how men are born,
And are all descended from these little bodies."
That was how Christ spoke when he looked at them
And then looked at me.
We were at the summit of a bump on the land, somewhere
With no light, no clear path.
"Distance from God, that was your inheritance", he said
To me, and embraced them again sadly.
Now Christ brought them on, walking with them and me.
The air cleared, the sun shone,

An open clearing of life and living things revealed itself before us.

35

A place of water, clear skies, peaceful animals eating foliage
The upper atmosphere conceals space, vast space
And an electromagnetic field spreads outward,
Deflecting the suns rays;
And a thin barrier of ozone,
And lighter gases which rise, but do not escape into space
Because they are
Pulled back by gravity and the coldness of space itself.
Space is absolute zero temperature, almost, so things freeze
What is zero? The distance between water freezing and water turning to gas
Has one hundred increments
And from water freezing point, to the coldness of space
Is two hundred and seventy three increments lower than that
Call that temperature at which water turns from liquid to solid zero.
The human body under the tongue is thirty seven increments above zero.
The atmosphere protects the earth.
It is a layer forty miles high, consisting of depleted oxygen.
Down here, there was a savage competition
Among flowers and plants, to get sunlight, water and soil.
And a profusion of animals, some enormous.
My guide and I walked through it.

Now, here, we find an enormous crowd
Gathered in one place, perhaps enough
to populate all of England, many millions of people.
Behind us, under us, the suspicion of a great lake of raging fire.

"Because the life was God, and what is here now of life
Is only what is Godly
And if any person did not want to see God before, they cannot see him now
And are lost, painlessly, mindlessly, in the lake of fire
The roiling mass of atoms.
Everyone else is here.
The world is logos, it is meaning,
And it is the law set out by God
If you didn't see it before, then you don't see it now.

And what meaning they found and made happen in their life is written in the book
In their minds and lives as they lived them.

"Where will all these people go?" I asked.

"They will move faster or slower, through Judgement
With a final aim in mind
To meet with God and be resurrected with him" my lord said,
"But first, see how, in the new light unaccustomed
We move toward that point there,
A single point of light, there, see how Judgement begins."

There was a single point of light
Above a place on the land.
It was a cave, where the people went by and gathered around.
Inside, the baby, the Christ, with the God bearer, his Mother.

"The first rule of proper free people and justice,
The greatest rule for people is, that you are held innocent
And have to be proven guilty.

People who did not have any understanding of Christ,
Can find themselves guilty here.
They will be judged and be punished,
But the punishment is only this,
to stay here with the child and his mother,
Until they can move on
Having understood.
Where they have turned him away in life,
so they cannot turn him away here."

"How long will it take, to learn?"

"Time is in the eye of the beholder, of course."
"So it is a race to the end again, toward Heaven,
By those who want to learn. If they don't want to learn,
To be what they were made to be,
they may stop by the way.

Or turn back, to the lake, I suppose – though few do this."

Let us make way to our God, the child, and grow up with him
As proper humans.
"Will it take 33 years or whatever?"
"It will take seven days, if there we can learn
and have no great sins to undo or come to terms with.
It is a matter of coming to terms, understanding, repentance.
And where you can find no guilt, there is none."

We saw the cave and the cradle.
I suppose you should call this day Christmas or the Nativity.
"The commandments of Christ, and the faith in him
Are the law of creation and humans
Written in the book of your consciousness.
And in the world.
How well did you learn and become a reader of this?"

And so, in an orderly way, at a time of peace
With plenty of time to spare, just as it was when Christ was born on Earth
When the Romans had established their empire, after the civil wars
And made the world propitious for universal commerce and travel
So judgement takes place, after the end of the world and the apocalypse.
Whether it was like Italy, Constantinople, or the Third Rome of Moscow.

36

I don't know if I should have said, that God had abased himself as a baby
And then immediately become a toddler,
He was a baby, an infant still; an infant and creator of all things.
Christ was watching himself, as in Dickens
The old miser watches his young and older self.

Now, there, imagine all those crowds dissipate at evening,
And my guide and me woke in the morning of the first new day.
We were outside the cave and the place where the child was

There were various people with us, but not those millions.
One was Charles Parnell. And he explained to me what was holding him here,
And why he might spend so much time here.

He said to me, that he felt he had a lot of guilt about his failure in life
So close to achieving his aim, too.

Over incredible periods of time.. who knows how long it might seem to him
We observed the child and his mother, and a father also, Joseph.
How she held the boy, and I must admit, I really wanted to see my own
children so badly.
The child was playing, moving about running here and there, beginning to talk.

And Parnell said:
"I am doubtful about how it can be, that Christ is born again
.. It is like another chance to be with him,
To follow and be with God in that way, which we can understand
And it need not be for centuries and thousands of years
The waiting about, for something to happen, to change
Like it is on a battlefield, where things are going on somewhere else mostly
Over a hedge, beyond the roofline in the next street.

But.. And isn't speeding up the time also sort of blasphemous?
.. But not to me.
Why didn't Jesus come to me as a fully grown man, and just teach me?

But of course, these objections are those of a man, me

Who resents how my efforts were spoiled by the way the Church
Turned on me, my followers rejected me
When it was revealed, that I had been having a secret relationship with a woman
The wife of an army officer.
I have to come to terms with that, my fault
That I could not live an ethical life.
There was love and devotion, and we married.
But my decision to love that woman in secret
Before her divorce and marriage to me,
Meant in some respect the failure of the Irish home rule.
I cannot accept that I did wrong. But with time, maybe I can see,
that the home rule, and the illicit love were imperfect."

There are limits on how fast something can move.
The propagation of electricity is at the limit of what is possible because
The speed that light transmits through empty space is the same speed

That electricity moves in nature.
Or else in lightening, or in little sparks of small lightening from some clothing.
And naturally, it is found in some fish which give electric shocks, like some eels.

On large scales, it is generated by movements of clouds and sky objects
Which fills clouds with charge. What is electricity and its force?

What binds the smallest things to one another
Is electricity. It is electrons
Little binding forces.
They are disorganised, and they do nothing except bind atoms
One to another.
But, if you're able to arrange them, face them the same way
And make one pass on its charge to another – if there are excess electrons
Waiting about and organised, then that's electrical force.

Electromotive force can be made to move through metallic wires.

A large quantity of electrons, relative to a small quantity of them elsewhere, is
measured and called voltage.
And if they start moving, they move either one at a time, or many at a time.
The number which move is measured and called the amperage.

How many will move at any time is determined by what stands in their way
Which is called resistance.
This is how you learn to harness electricity, and make it work.
You can make electrons form into useful groups, with a generator.

The final days of the world were dominated
in every way by this harnessing of electricity from nature
Making disorganised electrons behave in an organised way
So as to make them do work.

"Did Christ teach us this?"
It was someone sitting outside the Cave of the child
Which now was the hut, the tent of the family
On the surface of Earth, a place reserved, for a family in a town
A space for their tent or rather temporary home.

And also this man, "I am that one of whom Nietzsche said
That Christ's religion was the popular version of my teaching"
"Platonism for the people? So, you are Plato?"

"What is true is, that Christ put into practical reality
What I saw, prefiguring, like a Hebrew prophet.
And yet, I'm here, studying life. Having had no family"

"Why is it necessary to have known a family?"

The hymn of Christmas Day is heard.

"A soul has eternal life, as we see
And the soul has an eternal pre-established mind
And a life has an eternal pre-established pattern.
And a father and mother are essential, they are the form under which people are
born and grow up
The father and mother is an idea, realised in the perfect family.
Who has not seen a mother and father, has never seen perfection
And so cannot become perfect.

The discipline of the family home will last for an eternity for some
Who refuse to know it, or cannot understand it.

The idea of the love of mother and father has to be in the mind
For your mind to be right
And reasonable.
How can you understand love without seeing mother and father
And their immovable care for the child?"

"What is love?"
"Try this: overcoming all obstacles in order to remain loyal to the ideal
Of looking after someone. Treating the world with absolute disdain
If the world gets in the way or mistreats us
So that we can also look after and protect something
Including God"

37

"It's still a roiling fiery lake out there,
If any of these people facing judgement
Cannot learn to understand the Nativity.
They will either wait until the final ultimate end, here
Or go back, and be lost and consumed by the fire."

So said my master. He pointed back, to the edge of the land
Where the sea was. It seemed fair to me,
Who missed my children so much, to put such weight on the understanding
Of how God became a child. How the God is in the greatest
And in the most immediate and weak,
The most helpless, hidden under the appearance of weakness.

The birth of Christ is an easy happy time, for little children
The innocent, who deserve every chance
Whose innocence is like the innocence of Christ.

"What lake of fire? How punished?" I said.
Isn't this the resurrection, and the final life
And the Earth's collapse and evils all gone?"

"This is no final end, here. This is merely a point for the many
To learn to understand that the nature of the first
Is to be last and the last first.
This land here, is like an oasis of peace upon the lake of creation's fire
Roiling and burning around us, where the truth can be learned.
The world is still being folded up, and see that most of this place
Is almost entirely uninhabitable, and full of things which want to hurt.

These seas of fish and lands of pre-extinction animals.
And see all these people who despise the idea of family, home, country, loyalty
Not to speak of the other things."

Now, here I saw many people, who had understood what was to be learned
And set about coming to terms.
They had all the time and all the space they needed
And they very much wanted to avoid the fire,

Especially the giant reptiles going about their business in the sunlight.

I did not make my way aside from the lord, my master,
I did not want to get lost in the crowds.

But coming from the bush and the heat
Was a person I knew very well, from having written my book on him,
A book completed just before he died.

"Hello, do you know, they blame you for the undoing of all the West's values.
I never read your books like that," I said
Speaking to him with undue friendliness;
I took his hand in mine, warmly, and bowed to him.
He was that French and Jewish man
The most famous intellectual of his time, Jack Derrida.

"I never dealt with any of the issues;
I wasn't interested in the actual politics.
Like Bob Dylan in that way.
I didn't want any revolution, but simply to revive what had been valuable
In, in fact, Christ and God's creation."

"Why are you struggling here, to come to terms with childhood and family"
I said.
"I am not," he said. "I am moving on".
Perhaps he was ahead of me. In any case, he disappeared, taking a path onward,
away from the tents and our place.

And Queen Victoria, who had overseen a kind of standard of family life.
She came to make her peace with the child,
Alone, without crown or orb and that paraphernalia.

"Women ruined the land with their objectives in public life,
Voting for fixed selected candidates – as if that idea had any merit.
And their opinions are as a consequence listened to, in opinion polls
As if anyone told the truth, or even knew their own mind!
Loss of children and bearing capacity, with their pills and abortions.
Equality enforced is tyranny.
They build no homes, and give no place to children.

The children dead in those hospitals, and starved of affection
in the electronic self-obsessed world of working women
Who pretend to be men"
She would not stay for long with us, and was off – with nothing to learn here.

I was left alone.
Various stragglers came by as I sat and waited.
But night never came, sleep would not descend on me.
Time passed, but I found myself unable to move away,
But remained contemplating the child and his mother, and the paternal man
who watched them.
Some members of the IRA, and the US Irish
Some producers of whiskey – that drink which made men happy together
And ruined marriages with violence; they came and went.

Miners from Wales, who were always with me for some reason.
I reflected on my home life as a child,
And on the raising of my own children, which had been such a failure.
Despite all I had tried, the amount of effort I had put in, the loyalty and
suffering.
And still there I sat, unable to go on; watching the happiness of that infant
With a weakness in me. My body weak
My heart sick with loss of my children
Mulling over why I had married so badly, and how it had been my fault.

38

There is no way of confirming the exact age of the Earth or of the material world.
When it ended, it was supposed to be around fifteen billions years old.
Such a thing is meaningless. Years are measured as a cycle of the Earth around the Sun.
When the material world was formed, there was no Earth or Sun.
So you could measure it with a wrist watch. Or the ticking of a clock
Which emits electrons regularly, or atoms, as a substance degrades
As the nuclear forces in it degrade regularly.

But that indicates little more than, a regular atomic activity.
How fast or slow or meaningful the empty ticking is, can't be answered objectively
When we cannot die, and we have infinite time.

It is long enough, to be alive.
Our imagination is made to understand our place and time for a life.
The Christ child, the Son of the maker of the world was at his home
Night was falling for me.
I had kept silent – I would tell you how long it seemed to me to have stayed there
But let us not speak of myself, and my pains, my boredom and restlessness
My wandering mind, like the mind of a man in a jail cell.

The Earth was well formed, and around us was green vegetation
And bees going here and there pollinating,
For plants need pollination where they have flowers
This allows them some freedom in their reproduction
And difference in the parents of the new flowers.

I hear Christ speak, no solemn words, but just this:
"The rule for children is, leave them alone. They will learn by imitation.
So leave them alone. Leave me alone.
And what about parents? Leave them alone, too."

We were at home; in the happy solitude of home
Nobody is allowed in, except the owner of the house, the dad

And the Mother
"Man is in charge", but women shall be respected and given tolerance and love.

Now my master said: "The church can come to the house visiting
And hear confessions. But the home is encouraged as the absolute private.
And man and woman must build it together"

I was outside, looking in, sat, waiting.
From time to time people had come by
Milton, John Milton, And Tolstoy and James Joyce,
those greatest of writers of the family.
"Where did the idea of the lost son, the dead son, come from?" I asked Joyce.
Because in his work, Ulysses, Leopold Bloom
is in mourning for his son, Rudy
Who died ten years before.

He told me: "I left the British Empire, when Dublin was the second city of
Empire.
And I know you, who yourself were so often desiring to leave yourself
To leave the threats to your property and your children.
Looking inside, Britain seems to have colonised itself
Just as it colonised the Irish once.

You knew the persecution. Provoked and at the request of a mad woman
who in any other age would have been confined and ignored
or, better, made to respect her husband, she would have
Let him care for her, as you did care for her.
There's no guilt here. No guilt in divorcing that woman.
But, she had the use of the state's powers, and madly used them against you.
So that, in the end, you knew how bitter it is
To never see your son
To be defeated by the country, and prevented from living with your daughter
Seeing the mistreatment of the next generation
A nation's young."

"But I never was an exile" I said. "I stayed. I lived to see my children
And my time with them spill and drip away like water through a Roman clock,
Spill, pass away, like sand in a water clock, or an hour glass."

I was consoled to meet this man, whose work I considered so great
And he reminded me that I had done wrong only
When I married someone who would never have made a good wife.

Joyce, who had his own problems, sat down also.
Night came on. The day ended. I slept.

39

There were not seasons of the year there.
The first day. I had lacked a family in life,
Now I would learn.
We were the wretched of the earth, I was a prisoner
Under judgement. By myself
I had failed myself. But so had all of these.
"I do not say, that it was a matter of turning your back on the world
And attending to family life and the home.
Men and boys leave; not everyone who leaves home
Is subject to guilt and judgement and sentence.
But you do have to know, that you are only flesh and blood
And that what is most honest, most true, is a father, mother, and children.
We can't stay here, outside the little city in Nazareth for ever.
It's not something to enjoy; having a family
It's something to undergo
It's the law of nature and therefore of God.
Who will build the walls of these houses? "
My master and friend said this. We saw them start work.

Put to work, to ensure they learned, were some men from across the world.
Men who often benefit from killing their children in the mother's womb
So they, the fathers, will not have responsibility for any young.

Old SA men from Germany; and Redrow builders
Who built those box houses in England,
Building all over the place. Building, living, learning to be a man and endure.
And the interfering Police forces of Cheshire were there, men and women
Were there, clearing forest in a gentle climate
Sweating. It was morning of the second day.

Now, for us prisoners, ashamed, there was the Duke of Wellington
Strutting about, Prime Minster, and minister of state
Anglo-Irish
"How did he get to be in charge, even here?" I said.
"As well as being Commander at Waterloo, and Prime Minister of the young
Victoria."

"Belongs with the scum of the earth, too, he does" my guide told me.
"Belong with those without a good home and upbringing
Who made such excellent soldiers."

Here, on what people at home would have called a tropical sort of place,
Among rushes, and palm trees, and flowers, streams by the sea,
The sinners of all kinds spent long or shorter periods of years and decades,
Learning peace, calm and order of a home.
They go under the lintel, over the threshold, to a fire place, a kitchen,
All a barrier to the roiling lake of fire.
All a barrier to the empty intentions of the surrounding non-world.

I saw the young Christ Jesus, with Father and Mother,
Playing out in the street, and that was the street
We were supposed to be building.
He took trips to the synagogue.
And this is man's fate.
It should never be in the palm of the hand of the government.
In fact, there was no king of Israel in his day.
And, the foreign rulers were considered usurpers and thieves.
Here is a bedroom, for parents.
Here is a place of play, dreams, sleep, care for the child.

"Some say, the government powers of the nation allow this space
But let us no more speak of that.
See how a democracy can become a tyranny of a large or small group over a minority.
How the democracy can try to become king inside a man's house.
There was a group which wanted to make the state into the parent of humans.
Every generation of English people and Christians had to push back against this demonic urge."
That is what the good Duke said.

40

And so the second day went on.
"Do you know, that the material world is formed, mostly of empty space
But, electrically charged, it feels and seems full
To the eye and the hand.
And every part of it, every atomie, is a small point surrounded by space,
Just as the stars are distant, small points. Bound together by electrical charges
Atom is joined to distant atom to make substance.
This applies to the lowest lightest atoms, Hydrogen, with a single first particle
It is also true of
All the other types of atom, which were made when
Single first particles were crushed together under intense pressure,
And that crushing and the subsequent bonds, which make different types of
material substance
Requires a nuclear force, much stronger than electricity
To hold single first particles together to make an atom
Which in turn, can join with other atoms to result in substance.
There are around one hundred types of atom matter.
Gold, iron, copper, salt, oxygen, and so on.
These are the elements; unbreakable, foundation of material things."

We were allowed now, to walk, and we went with the boy child
To see the gigantic herbivorous reptiles, pulling leaves from the ground, and
trees.
Slow,
We walked about, following the boy around
And he was aware of us, the child.
The child Jesus knew my master, and he knew his own role in the world.
Wandering into the bush
Exploring. "Is God like a child at play?"

"My people set out to the furthest corners of the world, a trading class
In Hudson's Bay in Canada, they set up an outpost of British life.
Always calm accountants, after money, taking nothing seriously, least of all the
natives
And they built their homes and took their uniforms with them,
In the disorder and the strangeness – to set up home anywhere."
That is what I said to my master

Thinking of how I had started to make home here
In this perpetual Christmas, to recognise my faults
And my guilt. "Ah," my master said, in reply,
"Or what about the hill station in India,
With its little church, its mansion house and veranda
And the suits and hats, the women with their parasols
An island of England in India, or anywhere, far above the locals.
Balancing the books, and keeping up the home customs."
And I replied: "They set up a little bit of England
In some corner of a foreign field, when they died, too.
Travelling around and building home where they found it."

The boy makes his way out, and we follow.
"Do any people need to come with us,
to expiate in long years and thousands of years of learning
About how to be a child like this?
How much of a terrible thing it is, a human being
And to fail to become one. How it ruins our eternal happiness"
I said. "The child is almost worse than the wild animals
For the punishment it can inflict on me." I said.
While we were talking, one came out of the bush.
He had tried to escape from the space where we were
Whiling away life in the domestic clearing.
"There were thousands out there in the forest,
running into and running away from the dinosaurs.
Bloody dinosaurs!" and looking to my master, he said:
"So, we either stay, and celebrate this eternal Christmas
And learn to be loved by God,
Or we end up in the guts of a terrible lizard?"
"Yes, that is how it is, it seems" I said.
"And who are you, coming from the forest,
Having tried to escape?" "I am that clinical psychologist
Obsessed by the closing down the public space
And freedom of speech, and reason
Dr Peterson. I have no wish to evade my sentence
Nor to give up. But, I did want to see
What goes on outside our safe spaces."
"What did go astray, what went wrong in the world,
Do you think?" I asked him. We had time to talk

"We have fashioned a land fit only for the old
The spent, The stuff of old men. All old men.
They said it was about a new world
And further bringing down of barriers.
But it was just people unwilling to believe
In what counts, in man and woman.
And others, who were tired of living
Who wanted everything to be pulled down.
Everyone had grown too old.
The danger of reading history and myth is,
You once more enter worlds with aims and spirit
And, people with imagination or with education
Find themselves like children with ambition
In that old place where we were actually born and live."
The doctor sat down and was quiet.

My master, took my hand, at length, and led me away.
I gave my regards to the doctor, and we walked.
"The uncreated light of God we see in meditation, and
Is the energy of God himself. And natural light, that is created.
And do you know what light is?
Its smallest particle is the same thing
as the particle which carries the radiation,
the magnetism of the charged compass needle.
It is intrinsically bound up with the human mind and perception
For the world is not separate from the man.
Not separate, because man is made of atoms
And not separate, because the world is made to be grasped
And revealed by man's mind. Its structure responds to his grasping for it.
He gives it meaning and existence.

Material light consists of the photon
Which is emitted in a packet, from a source
And has a position, like a dot.
But it can also be understood as a field, not a dot.
A field and wave is not a barrage of photons
It is a motion, without parts of any kind
An influence with not point position
It is a thing with no mass, no position, defying understanding.

The intensity of the photon wave, the quantity of points pouring out
Is their frequency, how often they come out of their source.
Low frequency light is called radio waves,
And high frequency light can be seen by the eye
While the higher levels of frequency are enough to cause heat and burning
And the highest of all knock molecules apart, shoving their electron bonds off."

 "Why do you teach me about the rudiments of nature
Which I enjoy learning and understanding?"

"Because after the apocalypse, and this judgement, there is resurrection
And God has made the new world the same as the old.
And the way God made the world then, is the same as it will be."

41

"Is the world still being gradually turned back on itself
Time going the other way?"
"The great scroll of the world, the paper all creation's story tells,
Is not yet rolled entirely
And so continues to go back, to the origin of creation",
My true guide said to me.

"But now, the great lake of fire is at work,
And the place is inhospitable, uninhabitable by men.
The world without men is a pure spiritual fire
Of immediate unmediated Godhead.
Like the noumenon under perception and intellection.
So, it goes on around, while I bring for you
A clearing and space in which to learn and see.
Though each man is, as it were, alone
Like a monad, with me, sometimes.
My father wants you to stay close,
And make you able to see him,
Where you failed to do so before
In life." We walked back to the scene of the boy
And his family, but, I felt that we were going to leave
Ready to leave now. My master pointed out somebody to me,
"Here, see. It is the solitary, the one who knew himself the most
The German, Nietzsche; him who was your master first.
In thinking." It was him:

"I have paid attention to this boy, I have followed him
And seen his presentation at the Temple. Did you see it?
If you didn't, I will tell you.
How I, the foremost atheist, the man of the statement 'God is dead!'
How I got to be here. I understand
That anyone who is aware of thing greater than himself,
And is aware of a God-sized hole in his life,
Will be found here, in this afterlife.
And I certainly belong among those people.
At first, having been resurrected, I wanted to leave it all.
I wandered away

I was eaten by the large lizards. I jumped off the cliffs.
I starved myself. But our names and our fates are in the book of life
And we are brought back. God, apparently, knows what is best for us,
And this is our punishment: to be unable to die."

"Have you been here for long; did you see Christ the boy,
Going to the synagogue alone?" "Yes, he goes there alone.
And it is this that I have to get used to, and to understand,
That the maker of all had a home and was human many years,
With a mother and a father, and four walls.
I despised all that, of course. And I failed to find my own wife, or have a house.
My later madness, seal of final victory to relent or come to terms,
Was mostly an unreal dramatic illness.
Just as my laughter at God was also histrionic.
I have been here for ages, centuries. My fault is
I do not want to cease to exist, to give up.
And I do not want to accept alliance with a greater mind than mine
Not yet.

And my master addressed him, like this:
"You very well understand the ultimate aim of God
To make you have faith in him, and to make you love him above all,
To make you see him in yourself,
To force you to learn to love beyond your personality.
But you can't get past the foothills and go onwards?
There are twelve such tasks here."

"It is obscene. He forces himself on us!" he said.

"But you have tried to get away. It is horrible to be trapped and made to love
Against your will. But that was always the task in life," my master said,
"To let God draw you to himself and to transcend your limited experience
Of your own life." Nietzsche replied:
"I suppose that natural man, not the superman,
Would make my a natural situation such servitude."

"What is love, according to God? Or, what is love?
It would be coming to terms and accepting the conditions of life
And disdaining them.

Like stoicism. With focus on the inside, keeping steady, for time in eternity,
Loyal, unswerving." We prepared to leave him,
Daring man, Prussian soldier, impeccably intelligent, and the most hardened solitary,
To the limit point, that he either dared to go mad,
Or feigned being so to the end;
I took the chance to say something to him, but merely bowed and took his hand.
"I have had many dreams with that man in them.
I only began to take my eternal destiny seriously,
As a problem, and to study well my history and philosophy
Because of him."

And then, we walked to the Temple
And saw the place where the Presentation had taken place when Christ was a baby.
Here, we find Christ alone, disputing.
Here, sacrifices of animals take place, just like a slaughterhouse
But one in which the killing is done by a man looking carefully in himself
To ensure that he is pure enough to see and hear God,
Even if he is to get dirty in the spilling of the blood.
These Hebrew temple sacrifices are sacrifices like
The killing of animals by the Greeks outside Troy,
And like the Indians in the Rig Veda.
The organs are removed, the meat taken and wrapped in fat,
And roasted; the fumes rise up to God.

"But, notice how the priest meditates, thinking carefully,
removing his mind from the world
To put it before God!
That is prayer. The meditation and the prayer
Is that ancient frame of mind and attunement to His voice
Which accompanied the meat burnt offering.
The Temple was no mere slaughterhouse,
But the place where the priest set his mind in silent appetency, so as
To hear, to see omens, to communicate and listen.
By signs from the entrails, or bird movements,
Signs, voices, silence in the mind;
He looked to see or hear God's motions.

They are desperate to hear God's advice!

The Upanishad's prayerful meditation
Is supposed to derive from this Aryan rite of sacrificial offering
Which was always accompanied by a mental composure and
The desire to be aware of the most spiritual things.
And the Hebrews did it to.
They laid out the offering, raised the knife,
Silenced all merely human ideas (in the head of the priest).
Cynics say, that it was about getting the meat; murder.
Sociologists say, it was a gathering of all around an act
God, men, beasts, friendship, prayer. We say
It was the moment of most intimate union
Of God with priest." My leader finished.

"And they don't do that anymore, we don't do it", I said,
"Because while the prayer and the gathering and the eating together
And the smoke rising is the same, still
The sacrifice at Golgotha was made, the last needed by any Christian,
When the Lamb of God was offered.
All men, and at all times, can commune with God; no need for the entrails,
Just the meditation on the once for all offering.
The stance and attitude and attunement of the priest
As he studies the entrails, composes his mind to hear God's voice and guidance,
The spotless composure of his mind, and the openness to be captured
By the endless creator of all, this same mood is now available to any follower of
Christ,
Without need of meat offering, nor need of a communal ceremony,
Without need of the smoke of burning fat rising to the heavens
To be breathed in by the gods.
Christ made it a matter to be thrown back at the single individual,
The private person, the legal subject.
So, even the offering on the holy table –
"Thine own of thine own we offer unto thee" –
Points right back at a human being, in particular, you.
Above all, understand that the priest with the knife,
His mind composed, silent, seeking to be without defect and contagion
Of the pettiness of the world; released from the mind
Of the man at the breakfast table,

Who has to compose himself only to get on with a routine,
Who struggles to put back together a disorganised hectic life,
Every morning after the little death of sleep,
Unlike that man at the breakfast table, the Christian
Is the same man who sits and repeats the name of Jesus Christ
And offers a broken spirit, and looks for God in himself,
Looks to have the Holy Spirit visit him
As the ancient priest with the knife was
Looking for the Holy Spirit in the murder on the altar."

And then, we moved away from the temple,
And Nietzsche stayed there, unwilling to go back to the human life of the boy
child
And the little oasis in the desert, the solid ground on the lake of fire,
Our place of human life and the celebration of the Presentation,
A clearing of safety in the Jurassic and Cambrian era mayhem
Of dinosaurs and all that prehuman palaver.
Not yet. He would be stuck here for longer. But I was leaving.

"We need to move on. We have only the six days," my master said,
"On the seventh, I have to be at the origin of things.
We must get on. No waiting around with these old philosophers".

42

We left the home of Christ the child and the Feast of Nativity
And having been apprised of the child's presentation at the Temple.
While walking in the wilderness, we saw
The creatures which composed a whole kingdom,
About which I had heard already,
Organic structures, moving slowly about, populating the earth.
Their memory and reconstruction in books and models
Is beloved of children, who are fascinated
Knowing for sure that adults are not the biggest monsters in the world.

Gravity held them down, though in size they were made
As big as they could be.
Sea creatures are bigger, sea mammals,
Like those massive basking sharks; and whale sharks.
Animals on land need bones to lift them
And bones are harder when they're heavier
And heavy bones need flesh and muscle mass
Requiring heavier bones. There is a limit on the bone
And on the muscle that can grow
Specified by the bonding properties of atoms,
Which cannot be exceeded;
Simply, the atomic bonding of huge crystal solid bones
Fights against gravitational forces pulling the monster down
Until a size in reached where compounds and atoms in a body simply fail.

Without men around, the dinosaurs grew as big
As nature or the forces of matter would allow.
Mass is the quantity of atoms; count the atoms to find the mass.
And the gravity, a power dragging atomic groups to matter groups,
So that the force of the dragging gives weight to the mass.
And, just as an object moving exerts a force on another object
And both push against one another with equal force,
So gravity which pulls is the same thing as acceleration in the thing pulled.

Out in the wilderness and desert, a beautiful place, savage, bloody
But lovely, we were walking away from the oasis of calm of the first Christmas.

"Where are we going now, my master?" I said,
Gloomy because I sensed a long period of aimless wandering.
"To another refuge. Another examination,
A judgement", he said.
"In your judgement, in the place set aside for your punishment and repentance
It shall be what you require.
I know you. You, Jason, were the man without personality.
Just a function of your country, like a mirror
Warped a certain way, to assist survival of your country.
The surviving man.
Even such as you have a particular unique afterlife,
And even a prophet of people must be entirely himself.
(As De Gaulle said, of Europe,
There is no European literature, unless each country writes
And demands to be specifically itself, in Dante, or Goethe).
So, you are going to write and see only what is most particular to you.
Let us go".
While we walked, we were joined by a personality and style
I could not break free from in life; and never understood
So uncanny and at odds with mine. I knew him when I saw him
Because all the various images of our self we had lived with when alive
Were an amalgam image in the afterlife.
It was the first and the best of the poets in English for many hundreds of years
Thomas Stearns Eliot, who came to walk by us.

"Sir", I said to him "I know you understood how to pray
And that you detested and feared those bongo drums and the snake worshiping
of the Greeks
Which my master and I were just now discussing.
But what we had said about prayer in the mind of the priest with the knife
is the central feature of devotion in Eastern Orthodox church.
What do you say?" And my master added:

"When a saint prays, he is thinking of Christ and God
As the pagan priest outside Troy, was thinking of the animal and the gods.
That attunement with God is the same;
It is the bond between God and man."
Then there was quiet, while we went on, before Eliot replied:

"The Western empire fell,
At the time of Justinian.
While the West was in ruins,
In the East, prayer remained the ruler.
That new seat of empire in Byzantium, powered by prayer
Lasted for another thousand years after the fall of Rome.
How, but by a strict moral obedience, and binding of church and state
Into a theocracy?
Western Christianity went its own way, until the schism, and gradual decline.
The East, like a fossil, is still there, the same
As it was just after the days of Christ himself."

"Is it right to think of it as a fossil?" I said.

"For Westerners, yes."

"At the end of times,
There was no Church;
When people have no good from God
They find good anywhere and everywhere
Which is what Pascal said. When there is no God in their calculations
They insist on finding God in everything, good, bad, indifferent
Different from day to day.
And above all, they had no country!
No attachment to any land or any people.
So, when Dante spoke of the decline of Florence
He blamed it on immigration; the population had no interest in the land.
Christ had a country, and a people. This is not a historical accident."

"I feel
That my nation is my personality. It is my fault.
And I am punished for that here, or corrected, where there is no land.
 But what is a country, a nation?" I said.

"It is the same as a family, but with wider relative pool."

43

Around us, the animals ruminated,
The animals which breathe air
The oxygen rich at our level
Where pressure is high, where the air's weight compresses us into shape.
There are other gaseous atoms in it, like carbon dioxide
And some lighter gases. Above, 30 miles high
The stratosphere ends
And the ionosphere reaches out into space, alive with unstable
Charged dust and gas, and plasma, to 300 miles upward from where we were.

Plants started making oxygen in large amounts,
So mobile complex living things like us, were made to inhale it.
Plants used the carbon from the air as their food. For carbon is their body
They don't breath, and suck in the poisons we breathe out.

"How do we know what point of history we are at?
If history and time were a linear diagram, then where, now are we?
Going backwards, we're at a point in history"; this is what I asked
And I looked at my master, expecting him to tell me.

"Men worked out that the earth was not made in six days,
By seeing that all the surface crust of the planet is in layers;
The upper layers are the most recent, and the layers underneath were once above.
Layer or strata lie on top of each other
Some layers are from the decayed matter;
Rocks consist of millions of years of crushed soft matter.
Fish and sea shell, soil and plant matter,
Under pressure, forms rocks. The English worked it out,
English people like the Reverend William Buckland,
That where two things lie in the same layer of compressed stuff,
Then they are from the same era.
But they had no ability to work out how long ago each strata was laid down!
How long did it take, for instance, for a layer of rock on the bottom of the sea,
to rise to the height of a Welsh hill,
So that you can see fish fossils up there?"

Here we began to consider Christ in his country, Israel.
I do not know how long I had been now, going along with my master, the Son of God,
And TS Eliot, my beloved poet.
Before we came to another place of rest,
Many of these with me, people drifting towards us and away,
Decided to go off and die, picked up by the head in the mouths
Of ferocious dinosaurs such as the T Rex,
Rather than love their own native land;
The collection of people who gave birth to them as a tribe.
Rather than be reconciled with the conditions of life as a man
They would die.

And, Pericles of Athens, he was there
Him of the Civil War, or the Peloponnesian War
And that was what pained me the most –
The fighting inside a country.
And this is what he was thinking of, the last struggles in the world,
just like his, at the origin of the West
I asked my master for permission, to speak
And confirmed it was really him
"Why did the Spartan city fight it out with the Athenian?"
"Why did the French fight the German?
Or the Russian the Ukrainian?
They are often encouraged to do so, by external enemies of them both.
And, the loss ruins them both.
Just as the British fleet, the Royal Navy,
Never sailed in the same way again from England after the war:
They never again went out for wealth and brought it home
Because of natural power and right,
once the war had started and reached the point of the Somme and Ypres.
It broke the back of the two nations
It made them less scrupulous; it blew out the candle of faith in God."
Like some influence to destroy them both.
"Sir," I said, to Eliot "You were there when the British Empire was at its greatest power
And watched it all go under, piece by piece
But you wrote almost nothing about it.
Why is that?" and he: "I was not especially conscious of it at the time

Of Britain as a particular entity standing out amongst the others.
All the lands of the West had their overseas possessions and associations,
Of course, I could see, that civilisation and culture
Were in their last stages. I do think, that the insistence on England
Is parochial; it was simply their character, to sail to other lands
And spread out there. It was no sign of superiority."

And now it was night time. Why do people leave their country, in exile
And go to other countries? Why do they betray their people
As Alcibiades and Themistocles did?
Here those two were. It was dark, the night of the second day.
At least, these two did not betray some particular person –
but rather changed sides in a conflict
With the end of reforming their country.

And what is an empire, but the enforced
New nationhood on people, so that their ruler is overseas,
Like the British Raj – whose empress was in London.

But finally, what to make of those organisations
Which are national, but aim at colonising other planets? Like Nasa?
"I want to talk about that with you at another time –
About space travel, and its impulses and its future,"
My guide and teacher, and my saviour, said.

But I wanted to talk more about the movement of the planet
And the movement of plates on which we were walking.
The crust of the earth rests on a kind of sea of hot material,
A liquid, a fiery lake of lava, which comes out
And which can be seen on the coasts at Anglesey,
Dry and cold. Spilling out to the surface,
The layers and plates move about an inch every year
And push land up from the sea at the plate extremes.
Under sea there are great rifts forming and then the lava spills out.
So the continents move apart
And the Snowdonian range is all volcanic rock!

When I had passed by the two Greeks, the traitor
Alcibiades, who went to work for the Spartans

And Themistokles, who went first to Sparta, and then to Persia
To advise them and be welcome among people,
I realised, that they were at the outer edge of a new circle of clearing
In the wilderness of the Jurassic and Triassic.

This new clearing, where I found relief from the walking
Was described to me like this:
"Here a festival is being celebrated, always until the end of time,
To remember the time
When my mother, Mary, was presented to the Temple in Jerusalem,
She was made a maid of the place
As a sacrifice to God.
But not as an Immaculate Conception, which is just stupid
Meaning, that she was free from sin entirely from her conception in the womb,
An arbitrary dogma made up by the Roman church is recent years,
Like the dogma of the perfect knowledge of the Bishop of Rome;
Such are the new offensive unreasonable
And arbitrary demands made on my people."

Here, as we approached the centre of this space,
Were more exemplary men who had fled their country
For India, and built India: Napier, Lawrence brothers, and General Jacobs
"These are men who removed Hindu superstitions,
And created and invented and saved India
Who removed the Thugs,
So that Indians will always think of these white men
As the founding fathers of their modern nation".

44

Here, I found thousands of people milling around,
And at the centre, the great Temple of Jerusalem.
And, here they lived over again, the loss of Mary as a little girl
To the service of God, sending her into exile
From her family, to serve as a virgin in the Temple.

That was what was inside the clearing and the existence and transcendence.
In this area, this clearing.
Outside, the ages of the world marched backwards
At a steady pace, and I was glad to be out of the way.
The great monsters were diminished and gone.
It was such time as there were only the little animals about,
Or, let us say
They were not animals, so much as little heavily armoured sea things
These things which one day would crawl onto land.
I don't know, was it about 400 million years ago?

Men begin to shudder when they see such creatures
They seem to have no kinship with us.

Here, celebrating this feast, was Spencer Beynon of Llanelli
Who I knew in the Royal Welsh.
"My old friend," I reached out to grasp him by the hand
"Old soldiers, and sinners together, me a bit more than you" he said.
"I did die looking for God, and casting out the demons
And we meet here, at the feast of the Presentation of the Virgin.
Why here, Doc?"

"It's the place where we learn how certain ones of a community are
Offered to God, sacred, holy, set aside, accursed among men.
Us, who followed the colours, and did other more dubious things
We were set aside as
The accursed and holy warrior on behalf of the res publica.
What happened to you
When the world ended?"

"Has the world ended?" he said.

"Well, you know that I died before that, eight years before, you were at my funeral.

But how did I die before my time? that is what you want to know.

I came home, left the army, four years after you.

Went to Afghanistan. Didn't finish the tour, due to injury

But I wasn't feeling right. I was worn out. I was tired.

When I got home to Llanelli, I found myself alone

And too old to go back, even if I wanted. And it was impossible to find work.

You know how that is. I tried this and that, voluntary things

But they didn't like my personality!

I was not fit for any kind of social project.

So I'd wait for the nights, and have a drink of strong alcohol,

And then go to the graveyard, and talk to the ghosts.

There was no homecoming into the real world or Wales;

Wherever Wales went, I don't know. In my head more than in reality.

And then, the police started their work on me; got a reputation with them

Always different people, so I had no friend in the police;

They were all young, aggressive, winding me up.

Until I was more or less confined to being an outcast, a rebel in my own land.

Finally, I wanted to be free of my self; and the demons

The ghosts, or whatever it is, that makes people unnecessarily hard and inhuman.

I cut them out, with a knife, one day.

I begged God to release me from the world and its demons.

He did.

And now I'm here, at the cross, seeing as how,

This torture instrument, this martyrdom of God.

Is also the pathway to eternal life. I died with God on my lips

Even if most of my life, I was sceptical.

Do you remember, how we used to talk about God

As if he was the third between us?"

45

Our clearing, the place where they are celebrating the Exaltation of the Cross,
Because, when Spence and I had spoken, we had been walking
And had come to this next place of safety.
I said goodbye to my friend, and moved with my master.

Some individuals there, we found,
They were the ones who were extremely efficient
At getting all the world's resources in their hand
Like individuals outside the nation
And whom the state ought to have controlled
And yet, the state, in an act of self-immolation, aided.
Rockefeller, and Vandebilt
Oil and steel people.
As I look around, I see life spread out everywhere, living things,
Green chlorophyll producing factories
Nothing very tall or extremely big. But everything at a low level
Hugging the ground.
"Do you know how to make steel?" my master asked me.
"By taking iron ore. It does not present itself pure, but in rock.
Then melt it, cracking the ores open,
And pouring it into moulds to make shapes.
But the iron, an elemental atom, becomes steel (which is a compound,
Not a pure element
It does not appear on the periodic table)
By adding amounts of carbon,
For which use the stuff of coal. The carbon makes it rigid
But it has to be tempered, too, so that it sets with the correct freezing
Cold crystal shapes. Tempered, cooled down quickly.
How do you get the iron from rocks? You heat the rocks and it spills out.
And how to do you get such heat?
In a brick kiln, fed with blasts of air,
But how to make bricks?
From clay, and use coal to bake them
And the coal should be dried to burn hotter.

But you also need lime to make those bricks, and bind them together.
And you need lime. Lime is the thing! Where is that found and what does it

look like?
Ah. Lime is just the stone, the white stone, which will melt at high
temperatures."
Add lime to your clay bricks, and they will be strong."
"Why are these super rich, these villains
They used to call them 'robber barons', here?
Are they forgiven?" I said.
"All the so called great men survive. Those who lived
Live on here. But they are judged.
Only those who want no further life at all, are rejected
And go into the vast lakes of fire under the Earth!"
So he spoke, and smiled.

Here, also, Boris Yeltsin, the last ruler of the great power plant
The Union of Soviet Socialist Republics
Who took all the assets and gave them up for management by a handful
Of gangsters and men who were licenced to run little banks.
The oil, the coal, the steel, the gas, the aluminium
and other natural resources
He gave up to them.

"The aim was, to make the failing country Western.
Do you know, what the most important quality of the West's political culture
was?
The presumption of innocence." It was Yeltsin himself telling me this.
"More than anything else, this is the magic principle of a prosperous nation.
It allows the state to exist, and rule
But it allows the members to believe in it,
And love it, because the state is not allowed at any time
To take them and mistreat them.
The innocence of the person before the law of the state is everything
We never had that. Only England ever mastered this and believed it, and loved
it."

46

And here, at the edge of the sea
There was no monstrous sea creature like
A whale, or a great white shark, the sea was empty.
And on the shore,
They were celebrating the nativity of the God bearing woman, Mary
And her birth.

"We know she was presented to the Temple as a girl.
And we also celebrate her birth, then?" I said,
To my master, "Your mother, she was.
It is hard enough, for people of my genealogy,
To permit the mother of God into the churches at all,
But, that I am now faced, with her festival
For her birth. Why is that?"
"My mother, who bore me, is chief of the saints.
You should pray for God to share himself with you.
But she, actually bore God physically inside her.
She consented to that task. So, if you care for real
About God, and Christ, you will learn not to hesitate
To follow her. And, in addition, as is traditional
Call on her help when you want to ask God for something."
These ideas were strange to me. I prepared to remain a long time.

There were many men around here, unemployed like
Walking wounded
Almost like the whole British Army, at Dunkirk, or maybe at D-Day
When they formed and assembled at the edge of Europe's West coast.
But also those men who made the weapons they had, from British Steel, a big
corporation.
And even the men of the British insurance companies which also dominated the
world

And, Ronald Raegan, "Why are these all here, for this specific festival
Except for this: that they were men who were ignorant of the little girl and
baby.
Here are parents, and a woman in labour.
Here we were around when the Mother of God was born."

Now, that most warlike of US presidents, who put an end to the USSR with Thatcher
With ideas and promotion of the USA and Britain.

Among the soldiers, milling about, I saw my adopted father's father, Elwin.
And he approached me. And I wondered that we did not know
When we used to visit him, that life would turn out like this
So sure and calm he had been, and kind. But, almost the same age now
And having seen similar warfare in our lives,
We smiled and said nothing to the point for a while.
He started: "You are wondering, why these men
Linger around the Virgin's birth. And why they are in groups
Like guilds, or grouped in the afterlife according to their profession?
Well, we simply share the same problem;
there was never any proliferation of saints and minor deities in our view of it.
But, now I see, if you need to become a minor deity yourself
Then, it follows, that there are such, in heaven."
We stood and considered the problem
As two people who look at a machine in need of explanation or repair.

"What did you do in Europe?" I asked him, after some time considering.
He had never told me.
I had asked. He had only smiled when he was seventy and I only ten.
"You had two oak leaves. And the rank of Captain. Will you tell me now?"
"We landed somewhere behind the infantry; resupply convoys.
And worked our way eastwards to Germany through France.
Here and there, we skirmished with those socialists –
For the Germans they were socialists
Heavy duty state, state money funded it all; and no God.
Socialists, communists even. Their Brown shirts all poor men
They loved it, the masses, the poor.
And we were making our way. An army of free Englishmen back then.
small units held us up, Snipers mostly, for which I was honoured,
as they were removed under my command.
But, when we got near Germany, the fires and the aftermath of fire was
Everywhere, and this is what I could not talk about in life.
Our air force had dropped bombs from above.
The bombs were fire bombs, aimed at the houses and towns and cities

From which the men of fighting age were mostly absent.
So, the bodies we found all black, melted even
Were small, and had the long hair of women.
There were thousands of them, day after day in those towns,
Shrunken and boiled; molten and liquefied by the heat.
And I could never myself accept that they
Had been burned to death in large masses of dead
For any reason. And it was shameful, because our people had done this."
He smiled, and shook my hand, but didn't want to say any more.
He and his soldiers went on to meditate and thank the Theotokos.

It was late in the second day.
I was not able to tell how long I had spent there with those men
But we wandered away, and into the desert again.
The majority of all the life and living things
Are either little microbial viruses and amoebas
Which do not evolve at all in the normal way.
Which have almost nothing in common with us
Or, they were little sea creatures with simple bodies
Like algae, green sea matter. You would hardly call them living things at all
But there were the trilobytes, creatures with legs, and simple senses
And some kind of motor
And they ate, shat, and moved about.
Everywhere that the environment
Did not suffocate or burn them.
They mated sexually, most of them.
In the sea, under the sea they are, for in the water they took their oxygen
Breathing. They weren't on land.

47

The sun was sinking again
The end of the second day. "The sun", I said, "Is it a nuclear process
Which produces light and heat? Or is it electrical,
So the sun is a giant magnetic and electric field,
Throwing out photons, and heat
Spinning, organised charge. So hot, that it melts everything,
Just as extreme electric charge melts steel in a welding machine.
Or lightening, so the sun is hot and bright."

The sun went down, and the sky was pink
The colour of the atmospheric gases
when light is refracted or slowed down in it.
Just as a rainbow is caused by air which is thick and slows the light down
Just as water does, bending an image.

We were safe in the darkness as we walked
Because all around the Theotokos, and her space on the Earth there,
Were the orders of the Western church
From the time of the highest point of Catholicism in the West
Before its temporal power grew and spoiled it,
In England.
Men from these monastic orders, of such influence and order as the
Fransiscan, Benedictine, Domenican, Cistercian,
As in the Canterbury Tales of Chaucer,
And those orders of religious labourers
Which went to the altar and the cathedral
Which memorialises St Thomas.

The head of the English church has his cathedral in Westminster in London,
But also in Kent, Canturbury, for that is where the Christians first set foot,
sent by Pope Gregory the Great
And St Augustine came. First to Kent
Just as in fact, Julius Caesar first came to Kent, to the same spot
When he found the blue painted Canti and their wives
Fighting along the Thames with them.

There they were, bishop, Christ's representative,

And priest, deputised to do liturgy
And deacon, bishop's servant
Abbot in charge of an abbey
And Nuns and monks
Friars of the holy orders of wandering monks, official agents
There had been a whole society with these orders everywhere

"Sir," I said to my master, "was the social order better in the medieval age,
Better than it was in my time?
Is it God's plan, that all society should be Christian,
And was it my job, to help to make that so?"

And he to me: "That was the England where a Knight was the chief of the race
Accomplished in arts of war and education
And Chivalry.
It was the start of England as a culture,
That Holy Knight and his followers and supporters of every rank.
Land derived, land owning, a hierarchy of aristocracy.
Line this up next to the KGB society," my master continued.

And from the flaccid cloudy atmosphere, I heard another voice
"I'm Alexander Dugin", the voice said, "And I would like to add
To your reflections on the Christians of our day,
Having been one of them. Before the end
I saw my daughter murdered by car bomb.
For my philosophy, taught in war time.
They thought to kill me, our enemies in Westernising Ukraine.
And took my girl instead. A mixing up
Of holiness and thinking, with action and explosions
In which the last days of the human race became expert.
And I no less, perhaps. But there were pure and thoughtless murderers for the state.
Some of them also here, members
Of those state murder gangs.
And by contrast, and a contrario
Here are the secret gangs of those who trusted God
And worshipped him in secretive small numbers
Despite a nation's prohibition of their worship.
For is it just as much God's plan, for the Christian to be few in number

And to take communion from their poor clandestine priest in absolute secrecy
Under threat of imprisonment, trial, and death?
Or, finally, a late Christian empire ruled by Christians in far off places of
Empire,
Where the Church was no more than an apparent arm of the state, like the Raj?"
That man fell silent; he didn't speak again,
And later on I couldn't find him. "What is God's aim?"
I asked. The sun went down, night came.
I had no answer just then.
"God's not historical. In each era, you, personally, only you matter" my master
said said.
How could it not be like this,
When God put his son in a mere girl,
So that he was the baby of a baby?
I lay down, in the wilds, with the movement of people around the place
Where the Theotokos was, when she was an infant.
There were thousands of people, gathered around that place.

48

In the morning of the third day, we walked on.
We came, my lord, and me
On time's path through space backwards
To an era where there were no animals on the Earth
Or, none that I could see.
It was a treeless age, with chlorophyll in general absent.

But there were people here and there
Those ones who'd got this far. Having been dead once,
All in their isolated ways they lived and died,
Now they were here,
Having being pulled out of the grave, out of oblivion and sleep,
To see the destruction of the Earth
And to get involved in the divine hideous task.
Those who survived and struggled to go on
Had been judged by Him who made them
And here I found them, with my master.

And for many thousands and millions of years,
In this way they were ready to endure the unravelling of history,
The turning back of time to the year dot.

Particularly on that day's dawn, I found a certain type of man.
They were that kind
Who had spent their lives in uniforms
Working in groups for Ford or the German Werhmacht.
They had been uniformed, obedient, easily led.
Now they were here, and would be here down the ages, seeing in full.

At the centre of the crowds, as my Lord and I
Shouldered our way through the crowd,
We found ourselves at the Feast of Annunciation,
To celebrate the moment when the messenger of the Lord,
Announced to the fair Virgin, that she would carry
The Creator of all the world inside her as a pregnant woman.

Many many people had seen no justice in the claims

That women were intrinsically, utterly unlike men,
Thinking of women as servants or workers, or mere people,
More often as the objects of an obscure raw desire.
That's how they'd understood them.

And now the same men sat down with lowered heads.
The Lady was in the chapel at the centre of their gathering
Like the chapel at Walsingham, where the English
Recreated Nazareth, after a vision of her there.
There was silence and a dim light, like at the chapel in Norfolk.

In the mud and the stagnant pools and flowing rivers from the rain
Outside our space of calm, there was movement of living things.
"Sir, what is that going on outside? I thought
We'd come to an historical moment when no creatures moved."

"They called this moment, origin of mobile life, 'the Cambrian explosion'",
That's what he answered.
"If you were equipped with instruments and patience
And took them into the mud and looked in the pools, you'd see
Development of complex mobile things,
Creeping in the pools and on the rocks.
Why did they all at once start to have eyes and legs,
And little pincers and hands at this precise moment of hisory?" Christ asked
me.
"And why the symmetry and sexual bonding, all of them,
So complex?" He smiled, and asked me these questions.

I didn't know the answer; nobody does among the learned. I didn't answer.

Now, let me tell you about the people I saw.
Among the soldiers and the factory workers,
Inside that island just like Walsingham
As the Cambrian Explosion went off outside.

I saw innumerable working people
The type who fought the wars and did the work, and didn't grumble.
There were many banded together, the men of the trenches
Whose names and ranks are on the cenotaphs

At cross roads in the centres of any community in Britain,
Ever since that Great War, that one which
Britain should have stayed well clear of.

They were sat there honouring the Virgin Theotokos
Whose home was there for anyone to see;
They knelt and lay there, loosely bunched like men at break time;
And they were asking the Mother to intercede for them,
For it is known and clear, that
When she hears, she speaks for us to God. They are
Sat hoping to see the Virgin through the window of the chapel.
They want to catch a glimpse of her moving about as a mother with child
In a side room there in the middle of their crowd,
In that clearing of peace and life.

My grandfather was there, the one called Powell
With shrapnel in his head which made him have those fits they never
mentioned;
Some Nazi steel in the brain for all his life
To give him seizures even after war, until the end.
Even while he worked at the steelworks in Brymbo.
We did not speak, I saw him, looking for the Lady and her child
And learning how that woman, Queen of Heaven, Theotokos, hears our
prayers.
I never knew him, and I did not want to interrupt his contemplation.

And, a handful of others, who worked for me in life,
At manufacturing in Oswestry and elsewhere were there.
All masculine and friends,
And if he never learned of chivalry when he was alive,
Then I found, when he got here, if he got this far,
He would learn about it here.

49

Most hurtful to me, was to see De Gaulle there,
The Frenchman who hated England, though the English had a soft spot for him.
And who only survived to rebuild France himself,
because he was given a little part of Britain to set up his France in exile.
As I was given a little piece of space to work out my salvation here.
O here he was, and I "Don't regret that you've allowed him to be saved" I said.
"He embraced the Lady and France's Christian history and origins
when he invaded his own country with paratroopers,
and set up the new republic after the war.
I wonder if he could have had any help in rescuing France
Against the Americans and their orders that it disappear?"
I said. But it is not for me to comment.
The man himself, a giant and general who had seen combat many times
He didn't seem bothered to do anything but sit and contemplate
The mother of my master.

The waters were starting to move, we look at the rock pools.
I saw the little midget creatures, in the acidic waters.
"What is acid?" I said. "It is any liquid which has too many electrons, negative charges,
So that, when a foreign liquid or object is dropped in, that object starts to fall apart
When its own electrons are stolen from it.
And, there are also alkaline liquids
Which give off spare electrons to the object of their attack.
Either way, they break down the object,
Modify it, make it fall apart.
And at the same time those acids and alkalis are also stripped of their charge
Until they become neutral.
New compounds form in this process, which look like dead matter, changed and damaged.
Discovered by chemists, with patience, experiment
Observations, taking notes, in their laboratory secrecy."
He spoke of these things with me with pleasure
Because he and his Father had made the world
And "men have understood the creation, selflessly, with attention and honesty."

There we were at the site of the annunciation
Where the angel had said, for ever, as far as we were concerned:
"Hail Mary, Full of Grace".

We did not walk away, and yet we had to, for the days
When I would be able to stand around these places were limited to just six.
And day four was already coming. Night fell quickly on us,
It seemed to me; I did not need to sleep.
If we were to walk, we would leave these things behind in time as well as space.
The light came on the fourth day.

"It reminds me of where Heidegger did his writing and thinking
In the mountains of the Black Forest, at his Hut. I went there once, with my son.
I had also just asked Heidegger's daughter
For permission to use extensive quotes from his book,
The secret notebooks about Gods, which eventually made me a Christian.
Though he denied God in his overt writing, and that secret book, too.
Where would I find him, by the way?"
"H.."

"Arch conservative and socialist, national socialist" my master said,
"Not like the English conservatives, who don't want
The state powers to get involved in anything.
Rather, your Heidegger thought
that the state would organise the whole apparatus
Of the human being! What monstrous ambition and blindness!"
"But my master" I said, "he also taught, that
The self, the individual, alone is the origin of everything;
Of thinking, and meaning.
And these are the highest reality,
And they derive from the Logos and God,
Not from the crowd. A group of individuals is a crowd
But the crowd doesn't teach meaning to individuals
God does. Isn't that what he was getting at?"
And my guide said to me: "Yes, that was what he taught
After the disaster; after the welfare and safety state
Of National Socialism had done its best to make the world
Safe and sound for human being's inner being!"

"They made a mockery of God's creation and his law" I agreed.
It was dark, and we walked on.
After some time, I pointed out:
"I still do not know where we are going, or what map
Or plan we follow." And he: "Yours is the way of inner observation
And purity of conscience and self understanding.
When you are ready, the next level and the new world opens up."

50

We had walked on from where the Virgin had submitted to bear the child
And now, we came to another place
A burial chamber, an artificial cave like those all over England and Wales
Set up in the new stone age
Large stones upright; and flat stone on top.
Smaller stones filling the gaps, and a door way at one or two sides.
Finally, earth thrown over the top of it all, so that it is a round dome in the ground
To any one who sees it for the first time.

Now, this is where the Virgin was buried.
Again, there were people all around
And again, "it is not for us to linger".
Here is the British Army at home. Generals,
old officers, troubled NCOs and productive ones and privates
Here, some of them are lost and were doomed as soon as they came home.
Suffering from mental illness and angry about being alone
They die in silence unable to talk.
The mother is waiting here at home,
and a man must settle down with her and his wife
Because though the Army will make men kill each other
Back at home, this killing murder is a crime
To be held at a distance to make space for peace.

The British Army just throws its men into a country
Of traders and money, throws the soldier
Among people who don't respect honour and strength,
When they come home. And that is why,
The Lady has them gathered to see her, at the end.

And MI6, and other characters whose callousness is needed,
but which must bow to the woman and the home and charitableness in the end.

Here, I saw Charles Peguy, the Frenchman and poet, and conservative
Who led his platoon in 1914 in the first battle, of the Marne, for France
As a volunteer, and leading from the front, on foot because he could not ride a horse

No natural aristocrat, he died there in the first days.

He wrote about the theological virtues of a Christian
And how Hope is the best virtue of all,
Childlike and free of weight and responsibility,
Fresh in vision and always looking forward.

"Here also are the other poets of this kind", my master told me.
"What kind" I said. "The ones who are of the land and despaired of it,
Old wisened things, who despaired and yet had faith.

Geoffrey Hill, was there, who I had nearly met, just before he died in his
extreme old age.
And R.S. Thomas, who I heard speaking in Wrexham,
Brought to us to talk by his granddaughter, old in years as he was,
When he came to see us from his church in Aberdaron by the sea's edge.
"Grizzled angry old men; with faith but no hope,
not the childish hope of the woman,
Mary, who died and went straight to her reward for her service.
Why do the old men moan about the decline of their land?
See, it is all gone now anyway?"

Around us, a static single season of warmth. No polar ice caps here.
Burning hot it was, in Europe or wherever we were.
There were little green plants here and there
among the rock and the poisonous pools of liquid.

"How shall we eat or drink?" I asked.
Darkness was falling again. We left the men and the women of Britain behind.
It was time for me to sleep; at night, we could not see or move.
I was fed by the manna somehow during my dreams.

51

In my dreams, I saw a child, I had care of a baby
I carried her in my arms; and fed the child from a bottle.
It has been years since my children were infants,
and years since I saw them.

I awoke, to find myself lying on the ground next to my master.
It was the fifth day since we had been in the condition of judgement.
"This is not so much like judgement. It is not as I expected
Not like Michelangelo's picture of the judgement and Christ the Destroyer in
the middle.
What is going on?"

Someone else explained: "That those who are not fit fell away and died
And those others, who were fit, but unwilling to hope
Sank into the lake of fire.
And those whose names are written in the book of life who remained
They are here and hereabouts, for as long as it takes.
They judge themselves, they know what is right and wrong,
Because it is in the nature of men to be built on the Logos,
And to see the laws of the creation; and remember that laws describe
Those activities which things simply must do. And that law is
that they should chose always to love God.
There is no other injunction, everyone is entirely free otherwise.
And one action is perhaps as good as another. But when a man knows God
The action he must take becomes obvious to him. That's why there is only one
law.
Everything else follows."

We saw the cave again, the bump on the land. The burial place of the Mother of
God.

There were men sat around here, or lying down.
Men and women, I should say. We went among them
And the place was grassy like; the only things growing were little grasses.

The people were of the common people, the masses, so to speak.
The working class. That element of a society

which does the tasks which are repetitive,
and which are essential, and unpleasant;
and which resembled other tasks of the same kind.
Without which, there would not be food, or shelter, for a people.

They were from defunct companies and companies I had heard about
Private enterprises which the state sometimes took over,
So the government provided funds and leadership.
For Private Enterprise and unrestricted markets do not work
Without help from the state.

"Indeed, the state is the prop and the support,
The bank, for the private business.
Where money is the sole motive for the business
It fails; and its products run out; and people suffer.
A bad policy to begin with, to allow businessmen to run free
And, so the state exists, both to support the ruined people at the bottom
The delinquent
And also the rich at the top, who fail to provide."

The people and the bosses making money from them –
that is how it worked. These, here, were the people.
As many as the blades of grass.
There were a couple of people distinguished among them, here and there,
For a kind of saintly quality, who did not belong
But stayed nonetheless. One of them, I approached
It was Simone Weil, the young woman of France who converted to the religion
of Christ
And wrote the future constitution of a state after the Wars were over.

I approached her, sat down where she was, near the relics and resting place
Of the Mother of the Son of God.
"Can I speak to her?" I asked my master
"Yes, but not for long, she's doing contemplation.
She is not here in execution of her sentence, but from love."
So, I told her who I was, and she said: "I died of hunger,
Saying, that the people should be treated and respected each one an eternal soul
And spiritual meditation saves them,
So they ought to learn it at school. And the state

Should have prayerful eternal being in the soul, and the creation of the soul by
God
Written into its bill of rights and constitution
As legally protected properties of a man.
I have nothing more to say, now, please go on".

And, I saw St Augustine there, too. The bishop of Hippo, for whom,
The state or the city, would redeem the people.
This idea had its day, and had some sense where the people,
As they did in Europe and late Roman period,
Could not survive without the civil apparatus.
Again, I did not wish to speak to him in case of upsetting his mind,
But there were others, too.
I turned to my beloved friend and lord, and said, "As I understand,
In the correct polity,
The judiciary, the police officers,
The media reporters and propaganda, and church,
And the business and wealth making,
Should all be separate. Just as the person is.
Only the military should be bound
To the government and the crown".

52

It was day, the fifth day I had been there,
But the sky was not clear. A strange colour of the sky
Light refracted through layers of some gas
From the constant pouring out of smoke
Out of volcanos and hills and cracks in the ground.
The ground was not steady, parts of it not even solid
But open to the core heat and works on the inside.
There were some places where the Earth,
Still forming, was not especially finished or round
The spinning and the effect of the gravity,
Centripetal motion, not yet working in full.
It would be impossible to breath for long,
But we were not affected by those gases.
Meteors were not settled into their courses, either,
And comets which round the sun and earth
Were still making their solitary way
Tended to land on the face of our own wandering planet,
Exploding here and there, small and large

"Oh they throw up the ground horribly" I said.
It was Edmund Haley who saw the comet which still orbits the Earth now,
The solar winds blowing illuminated dust off that frozen block
Behind or in front of it
For the sun blows an electrical magnetic wind.
Haley saw, that the same comet which the Norman invaders of England
Observed in the 1060s was the same one which came by again,
Over London in the 1660s. It has a 75 year orbit,
Flying an elliptic course.

Here, the Lord's Transfiguration is celebrated by the people at their judgement.
"They are here to see your transfiguration,
But you are not in front of them, not you, because you are here.
Yet, they celebrate it, and they seem to see you?" I said.

"They see the light of God
And wait to see it in themselves,
To believe that man can have God's energy" he said.

The judged stood around, and did not see the transfigured Christ
Who was next to me,
Shining with the radiance of God and his nature,
With the energy visible and uncreated,
But yet the energy was there –which makes creation happen.
Like the Holy Spirit. And once
Three men saw the light around their friend and master.
We know who saw, and all of them went on to write of Christ in life.
Who stands around?

There were few. Christ pointed them out, overseeing the festival of
understanding.
"Here is my friend Peter, who described everything he saw of me to the
evangelist Mark
So Mark wrote it down.
Here John, the beloved disciple, who also became an evangelist for himself, very
late in life.
And there, James, who they called the brother of Christ, the son of Joseph, my
father.
Who led the church in the first days, in Jerusalem.
St Paul knew him well, but disagreed with him sometimes.
And again, St Luke wrote out what Paul knew, which he knew from James,
perhaps.

The three of them were there, the men who saw Christ, and who knew he was
God's Son,
And I could not make myself talk to them
So revered and elite. But all three of them had spoken to me,
Either in their writing in the Gospel, or by means of the writings of a student of
theirs
Who wrote down their words and accounts they had told.

There they were, those three, revived and under judgement, as I was.
"They are here, and want to be here;
They chose to do so."

"Will you speak to them?" I asked my Lord.

"Not now. Let them meditate and pray.

More important than me being near to them today
Is that they, by the Holy Spirit, have that spotless purity of mind
Which the energy of God gives, the more than human mind and faith.
It is the silent peaceful eternal power of prayer in the man alone.
Nothing is more valuable. A man is printing money doing this.
Putting away riches."

As if it were an after thought, or preparing for a better demonstration elsewhere,
As precursor to a greater thought, he said:

"God doesn't talk to groups, he does not speak
With people who have plans and parties to look after.
He speaks with kings, and saints and individuals.
Protest groups and interested parties, private businesses,
And so on, can dominate a land without a king and without saints.
And they will ruin the land.
The English in the old times, in the good times
For hundreds of years understood their nation had a king
Who was the ideal form of rule, and he was reliably admonished
And representative of the eternal holy Trinity.
They called that mythic king and ideal ruler Arthur.
That aspiration and that certainty of what is right
For this land, and this people, points the way."

53

We did not move from the site of the Transfiguration
Which could only be seen perhaps in the mind, and people do come by.
I began to see them, waiting, praying on their knees.
Those who needed the same confidence in God
That the apostles had, to see with their own eyes.
What were they focused on? Inward.
And how did they know that this was their task, who told them?
Now there I did see some angelic being. For, what were the looking at
When the Lord was by my side, and they were not looking our way?
The greatest curse is despair and looking inside, and looking for God
Gives Hope, loveliest thing of all in life.

"Let us move on," my guide said to me.
The contradictions are too great; they, in effect are looking at me
And at the light in themselves,
And, whether each man sees God in his own way,
Or each man sees an entire world in his own way,
Is too hard a question.
Let me tell you now, that there are only seven days here.
And we are nearing the end. The seventh day is the day of rest,
And complete re-creation."
"So, the creation is going on, as we speak? The new creation?" I said.

The sunlight was pouring through the air, all radiating in many frequencies:
Ultra violet, unseen, but working hard on the ground and the waters,
cooking them and the little things inside –
little hardly visible things you might find living on Mars or on the moon,
Alive, immortal, unsexed, dividing, spreading.

The photons were there, or the waves of electric force from the Sun
Come nearly two hundred million miles in a few seconds, always, more or less indefinitely
Pouring up on us, deflected by the ionosphere,
But that protection was unfinished.
Because the world's scroll and all the skies were being rolled up.

Who were the people around, looking

at the spiritual energy of creation and God? Civil servants
People printing the dollar. Employees of the state
after the crown had delegated itself to such employees
After it had passed from to the parliament of aristocrats
And had passed from the businessmen and traders,
To finally be received by the hands of professional statesmen,
Notably, Churchill, Winston.

Churchill, whose family rose at the time of James II,
To become the wealthiest of families, according to Macaulay
By marrying and saving, and careful business.
So that when he was a man in the 1920s, Winston was involved
in the state's welfare programs with Lloyd George.
Him and Lloyd George reformers. Churchill was there
Sitting, fat and old, sitting with his eyes closed
In Christian meditation.

I asked him if he was glad of his record in the later period of which
He ought to have been glad.

He said: "There was, as so often in the old life,
No way to do good. There are too many ways of seeing events
To many opinions, and no way of settling them
The right and wrong.
A man had to be chosen in the end, to resolve the irresolution and debate,
And then, he had to act and be tolerated,
While he and his ministers tolerate the opposition.
Now leave me to my silence."

Galya was here, too, my wife, not far from him.
I knelt down beside her and embraced her warmly,
And then again embraced her, but she did not yet get up.
"It is not time for us to be together, Jason" she said.
"I am in prayer here, and happy.
And I have been told, that I will be brought to you later.
And I believe this." I stood and looked at her with happiness.
She never prayed as she should,
But always with the voice of supplication and petition,
Asking for this or that. Asking to win money

On the lottery, or for some favourable outcome for her family.
"Even the Greeks understood, you do not petition
When you sacrifice but go quietly at the feast."
She brushed aside my impertinent comment:
"We are dead, aren't we? I have been worried for you."
She could not see my master at that time.
Perhaps she saw him next to her, all to her,
I do not know. "It will not be long," I said.
My life's love, who gave me a home,
And a physical intimacy of her body,
And her immovable kindness and consideration for me
Which I had tested too often.
She wanted a man, who was a bit strong, steady;
An English man, at least, a man who loved her.
I went to kiss her and hold her again
My master drew me away.

54

At Pentecost, Christ and I witnessed them bow down many times.
We were watching, and the sky was streaked with lightening as they made their promises
And asked to have the spirit of God. This celebration marks the founding of the church
Forty days after the Eastertide.
They bowed low, and over and over
Saying, Lord Jesus Christ Son of God, have mercy on me, a sinner
Asking to be filled with the spirit, and promising to do its will.

There were some milling around, at the edges
They got up and moved about,
Or came back to the ceremony of the Pentecost
Where promises are made to God
Just as they do in any Orthodox church. They stood.

The atmosphere of the sky seemed like it would be ripe
For electrical fires and lightening
Because of the strong winds and convection of air,
Making the waters and gas charged
All on the same negative charge
So that the electrical charge wants to find a positive ground again, and finds its way to the Earth
As lightning.

So the power of God they asked for, too. Those standing around
Included him, the cause of the end of the world for some
For others, the inevitable end. Archbishop of York of 1954
Was there, too, with Putin. The Archbishop had said
That it would be right to fight, even to nuclear war, if the enemy was the atheist Soviet.
It would be wrong to let fear sway the people of God.

But with Putin, it had been different. It had been better
If there had been peace authoritarian atheist West,
And his land of authoritarian Christianity.

Now Mr Putin, he with so much guilt,
He came to speak to me. For some, he had been the actual cause
Of the end of the world, and he was anxious to speak to anybody and
everybody,
As St John Baptist was ready to receive anyone in the waters
Declaring to the world.
And he recognised in me an open mind.
"We started the war which seems to have put an end to everything.
But the war began long before, when the West threw aside its scruples,
Principles, and above all, threw aside God.
Russia would not allow such a powerful force of nations to swallow it up, too.
Russia's mission had been to bring holiness to the world.
I really believed this.
So we had to fight in Ukraine, and defend our borders.
Say that we caused the end of the world, or not. It is not so."

And he went back to bowing low to God
And accepting the gift of the Spirit and the Church
Without regret for the defence of Russia.
He was permitted to see Christ there,
and put his hands out like a man trying to keep water in his hands,
asking for Christ to put his own hand there.
He did, and the President kissed his hand.

There also, the other war leader I knew;
He recognised us when he saw Russia's president acting as he did.
He was that short man of Welsh stock
who was born in Criccieth, and buried there
And led the British state in its final years of desolating war
in France and Belgium which ended in 1918.
I spoke to him, feeling he was my countryman, being familiar.
We had visited his old house not long before.
I approached him:
"Why are war leaders here, or politicians? Predominating" I asked him.
"Naturally, statesmen find it hard to love the church,
So much as they love their country. So they spend long here,
Making up for the deficit, and asking to be part of it.
"But did you love your nation?" I asked.
"You always seemed to me to love ideas and reform

More than the land itself as you inherited it."
"I brought in reforms, with my student, Winston Churchill
Many reforms for welfare, voting rights,
Care of the old and the unemployed, for sure
Making the state take functions of the Church.
Disestablishing the Anglican Church in Wales
But Protestants, in order to maintain themselves
As Protestants and not cease to exist
Must continue indefinitely to resist and remove and protest
Or cease to exist. It's a ticket to hell. But now is the chance for us to reform.
Not all protest is welcome. I recall that day
When a Pankhurst woman came to Criccieth
When I opened that village hall there,
Shouting about their votes. And the police threw her in the little brook that goes past.
The war was won. At such terrible cost to the country's money stores,
And its stores of chivalry."

55

"Tell me more about that, what you mean, by chivalry," I said to him.
It was growing dark yet again, and the end of the fifth day was upon us.

"There is so much that we can get wrong.
When we are in the world, politicians.
It was better for most to trust to the church,
Not to the already massive state.
So anxious to do and intervene.
Here are the best principles:
Keeping a strong aggressive military
And the principle of social welfare at home for your own people
And the principle of patriotic conservatism
And the principle that every man will be free to do what he will,
Unless it's explicitly forbidden.
These are all right principles. But who can reconcile them all?
Now, the chivalrous man, the Christian man and soldier
He might be able to do this; I cannot say that I achieved it,
What? Me, the man from the fastness of Western Wales
A land with hardly any people at all? I merely ensured we won or survived that war.

What did not survive was Chivalry,
As it had existed since before Dante's time.
It is a very harsh superior attitude toward any authority,
Refusing to compromise personal liberty
Or any principles. Defiance of all earthly powers.
But, a submission and complaisance, almost love
For the weak and the powerless and the oppressed,
Where the chivalrous man can be found to dissolve into tears
for love of his lady or his children
The disabled or persecuted."

"What of the love of country?
Or putting your country above other values?
Isn't that what the socialists hate?" I said.

"You think, because I am socialist, that I prefer

letting my country be subsumed by international things?
Then, it would have been the case, that we lost all control
And the small would be eaten by the big."

"Are we right, my master, to love our country,
our people, more than other people and countries?"
And he said to me:
"The way in which the memory of God will be revived
Is by way of the veneration of the saints of these isles, I mean, British saints.
Men aren't made to be international. They are tied by family loyalties; and this
is right.
A man who can't love his country cannot be trusted."

Meteorites or falling bits of dust,
Moving at such speed that they ignited in the atmosphere
And shone like little stars,
Were in the air; the space outside Earth was alive with these lumps
Which were not properly in orbit. Not moving in a steady direction
The direction of the orbit, they circle around a heavy body being the steady
condition.
At that time, there were many loose objects, debris
Shooting like falling stars through the misty close air
And coming to an explosive end on the earth.

And so there were alien bits and living things landing.
The men and women, sat bowed in the night, who were they?
There were many of the early settlers of the Americas
People who signed the Declaration of Independence, not altogether religious
men
It is well known. But, what they did not know so well
Is that they founded the United States on principles which they learned and
believed in
Which only Christians could have stated and believed.
The settlers of the American north, were fleeing England
Which was as well;
And they eventually took the British empire away,
After their revolution of the late 1770s
Even the revolution was based on English
Christian principles

and the example of the English Civil War for religious ideas
Was foremost in their minds, even if,
They had no real faith.

"All the positive virtues of action blossom forth from the great root
Which is the love of your specific native land and your people."

56

Christ judges by inviting us to the feast,
Forcing us, who are dead,
To enjoy what was not ours.
They stay or go, as they want.
But the unimaginable years and slow decline of the earth
The featureless expanses of the hot furnace floor of the earth
With little atmosphere, and a sky almost always dark and twinkling with stars
Was their alternative.
"The stars, and the empty space. It is all mostly empty,
Except for those subtle forces going along
And the dust in the middle of it all, swirling around.
Far too great for the human imagination to be able to picture
An inhuman place."

It was morning of the sixth day of judgement.
Honestly, I was disappointed to know that Josef Stalin was in the crowd I saw
Celebrating the Ascension, which Christ had given to these faulty people
Who had done wrong in life.

"When Christ ascends, what does he leave, but the self, alone, you?
And, each man had to take up Christ's place, and become the son of God. "

"Stalin was not a just man, a man who took God's son's place.
Why is he here?" I asked my master. "He destroyed the church in Russia,
All across the east of Europe.
It is not as if, he had some religious atheist view of men
And perfection."

"This the place where self-love has to be understood.
And the self-indulged are corrected, see.
How, by giving up your self, you are loved.
How, by giving up your self, you are granted your real self.

Now Stalin, he was doing God's work, without his being conscious of it at all.
And, had he known his true self, he could not have done God's work in that
demonic way.

God brought the chaos of the Soviet times;
for every ruler has been put there or appointed by God
For one reason or another. Sometimes to be resisted. And resistance was the point.

The self, the individual, is the conduit of every good thing;
this is clear. But obvious only to people
who can focus on their actual situation. As people. As being here.
Most people can't, by and large. Prayer focuses this vision.
Stalin was forbidden prayer, and God blocked his eyes.

Now, love of self is to treat yourself as God's instrument, in the end.
A man realises his highest purpose. To be God's instrument. He becomes a
Christian.
How, by giving up your self, you are loved.
How, by giving up your self, you are granted your real self.
So, as far as your own will still exists:
it should only operate within the bounds of reserve and control.
So, sexual love is only good with one person
For the flesh if uncontrolled must not control you.
And sexual promiscuity and adultery,
and enjoyment of carnal things randomly
is a symptom of straying from your self, and therefore from God.
Eating, sleeping, and gathering goods, likewise.
Called lust, gluttony, idleness, avarice, and so on.
The lower things become highest in a man lost. Stalin
Was the agent of God, in a mindless way. Now, over many ages, he can be
corrected."

Stalin, who had courage and persistence at least,
To face his Maker and deal with it,
Had learned and come through. He actually gave me,
As I stood next to my Lord, this information:

"The Ascension feast seemed to go on.
The fragments of the great British Imperial experience in India,
Flags and imperial manners, uniforms,
Architectural and engineering achievements were here and there
The East India company's evidences,

Where the British started to stray so far from their Christian roots,
Their monasteries and holy orders, that they found
The Indian meditation practices unaccountable.
And strangely unfamiliar, though these things
Had never been forgotten in Europe in fact, in the East of Europe,
But especially in Britain, the Brahmins appeared strange and unchristian.
The last embers of Christian spirituality went out,
When the slight fires of them in India were discovered."
"That was how it was for me!" I said.

57

When I had spent time there, I don't know how much time,
I went away in that awful place, alone
And saw another place of meeting, and a black man I admired,
That doctor and preacher, Doctor King. He said:

"Every living thing is made of smaller parts.
But every part is made of smaller parts
There is no limit to the study.
but what can be conjectured, is that there is a spiralling double helix of
chemicals
Inside every living cell. These are thought of as a map or instructions
From which living cells form and gather,
And every organised living thing has different instructions,

The strips of instructions pull part and split off, making a pair
Then the first strip of chemicals rebuilds itself, and the separate one as well,
Now there are two.

There is a certain magic in the fact that man has discovered this.
The attention to detail
Of the man who believes in God, who has nailed down the world so that
It is the world which God actually made – rather than a hallucination, a fantasy
Which is more commonly the view of the world,
Made it possible for twentieth century thinkers to discover these facts.
They took God's handiwork, and worked out what it is.

The spirals and maps come from somewhere; they are part of life.
Life itself, mutating, copying cell by cell,
splitting and dying, fusing and surviving, gathering and building,
With instructions to bind into complex structures and organs,
These cell strands build organic cells around themselves,
To form bodies of all Earthly life.
It started somewhere; evolved over a billion years into a man, into the body of
Christ."

We looked around and saw no signs of life.
The cells were in the stews in puddles and lakes, green and brown and red

In the poisonous air, and the continuous rain of polluted undrinkable water.

Here, I heard my master, Jesus, speak of the individual life,
For whom the entire world was made.

"In the rains, the disorganised messy surface of the naked globe,
There is an oasis of calm. There aren't any trees or water to drink
But here, see them gather, some people to observe the ascension of God's son.
That man, there, is the famous scientist, Albert Einstein.
He who solved complicated problems at the limit points of the physical world."

He was wearing a raincoat, and there were some others around,
Members of those black liberation movements and the welfare
set up by the politicians Lloyd George and Churchill
Who we had already met.

But there was also, coming toward me and my master,
An eastern man, of India, the prince Gautama Buddha.
And also, the extreme thinker of French surrealism, Georges Bataille.

Now, Christ spoke to us, he could be seen by them
He preached and said:
"I speak of the absolute value of the individual self, to philosophers;
How your self might be joined to God. The man alone, the single self,
Can be with God.
Christ is an individual, born in a happy land among a people,
But still an individual isolated soul. Not a race.
God is in the man alone, and salvation is of the single individual
Not the crowd.
How you have each run this course alone, and with faith and hope!
A man is guided by a people, for sure, in education, experiences,
But the Absolute indivisible is only in one person.
And yet, how can it be, that a person, a named individual, you,
Is yet brought into the overwhelming power of the creator of all life
And remain who you are?
Do you lose your self then, when I have said, that you must be your self and be
free?
Only the intervention of God as man could resolve this paradox and dead end.
My father resolves this paradox in me.

My father wants you to be part of him, and to be God.
Before, in life, it was possible in glimpses and moments
Now, after the death and resurrection, it will be so in full."
So he spoke.

58

The Buddha replied to my master: "Is not prayer or self-observation, meditation,
Until there is no trace of false understanding but only calm observation,
The kind that lets the mind be and go
The way to the Godlike divinity?"

And Christ to him: "That is so. But once again, people have taken you
Old prince, to have reconciled men with God.
They say you prefigured Christ.
As you have found, unity with my Father is possible.
And all those intractable virtues of honesty and intelligent observation
Of the ways of God
Must follow: to avoid vice; to maintain personal integrity;
to care for the poor; to ensure that there is order in society so that peace may be.

Prayer, people think, will reveal heaven. What?
A foreign place, an unknown unheard of vision
Which they will give to mankind? No. Heaven is here.
And even in Heaven, the moral injunctions and care over one's things applies."

The protestant ruler, the arch politician of the West was there
In his old armour. Cromwell was talking with me, as I sat next to my lord
Because he was English like me, and it is common for people of any place
To look for their like. And Christ, near two thousand years before us,
And from a distant sandy hot place
Sometimes seemed not one of us
In this unity of origins.
"You mean, sir," he said, "that there are practical ethics and responsibilities;
As when the Spanish and Catholics and the Pope, for political reasons
Because of a disagreement of principle and power
Would invade my country. And love cannot be infinite
Has boundaries. Is bound to a community.
So, my first responsibility was to recognise our enemy, in the Spaniard
And to set out to defeat him in war."

"And the same, for Arjuna, from the Mahaburata" said the prince.

Christ said: "Your loyalty to God is a personal thing
And there are no rules for when war is to be fought and how to acquit yourself
in war.
Because every event is unforeseen and unique. But a man must look after his
people and his family and loved ones. This never changes at any time.
He would be judged for it another time
If he failed to do what's right to protect the weak.
We call doing the right thing courage,
And praise success as valour."

Just so, the virtues which relate to God, in the individual alone
When in war or in peace, are the same.
And Faith is required of anyone who sees war,
and the failure of his ambitions and his community
Because such things are bound to happen."

I have seen men in training sessions in the army sat in the outside
On the ground taking notes, and this is how they were.
The rain sprang up again.
"Faith is simply this: to know that I am God
And when the moments of lost communion with me arise
To remember me, and to still believe, in the worst times and the best the same.
Faith means: seeing the point of existence, and its meaning
As that point where God and man join together
As they did in me once on Earth. And not forget."

There were other people arriving, little bits and bobs of people
From faceless groups, and radical individualists
To learn of Christ's ascension back to his Father,
In the festival of celebration to observe him
Rise toward the heavens and out of sight.

The BBC people, always on the edge of turning England into a socialist
nightmare
And Greenpeace, again, the greatest of organisations
And the worst.
And Sir Francis Drake was there, too; the imperial man.
All of them, on the edge of doing absolute evil
Unless they also had faith.

How did the BBC look, who were they? They can be discerned
As those modern British rulers, civil servants,
Confident, soft, refined in learning;
Not many of them got to these final stages
Of judgement while I was there.

59

Electromagnetic waves, which include visible light, and radio waves
Can be sent by any strip of metal, sending photons, little packets of energy.
Photons aren't stored in the metal; they are energy given to the strip antenna by
a source of electricity.
You can make the photons pulse like waves of water hitting the shore
By increasing and decreasing the power source of the antenna, in regular bursts
This makes a wave of a certain frequency.

An antenna some distance away, can be made to catch the waves
If it is tuned to catch them.
Information can be made to sit on the waves, carried along by them.
This is the principle of the radio transmitter and receiver.

The radio uses photon radiation, which is in principle composed
Of particles with no mass when they are at rest.
They move at the speed of light
The boundary condition of all communication in the universe is that speed.

But the voice of the world is silent, unless through light and the things we see
with light.
Light itself, is the same stuff I have just described
And, if you photons it at a certain frequency you get a hue of coloured light
And at another frequency, a different hue of colour
A stream of light slowed down in a curved medium
Will appear to be natural rainbow.

The voice of the world is silent unless it is in the visible light,
And in the material objects which push us here or there.

The voice of God might come to the inner ear of the individual.

Just as God makes the world anew every day
And even now sustains it
For the free man, what stops him from jumping into the lake of fire
And simply giving up.
Anyone who has seriously thought about this
That there is just oblivion beyond life, if he chooses;

And that there is God and further life, and the challenge of joining with God
Why would he chose the challenging way,
Unless he also has hope?
Things will always work out right and well
But men don't know this instinctively.
They have to hope that God has them in mind. And this too is a virtue
Which should be cultivated."

I was listening to my master speaking. And we moved on.
"Does God speak in the objects of the world, and in the things we can see?"

Walking with us, further back into time, to the very point where life began
In some swamp, or on some distant planet, so that it simply appeared and
sprang up,
In vast inimitable complexity, all at once, like sublime genius,
We came to the point where life starts,
beating, moving, in a cellular form, a single cell.

Christ bent down to let the watery mess slip through his fingers.

"Radiation of extreme frequency will strip an atom of its electronic stable
charges
And leave it charged improperly
So it goes about looking to bond and mate with others,
It is as if it has been cooked and ruined.
Such are the origins of life,
in just such a chaotic burst of violence and lightening, or some meteor storm
Where a strange bonding and cooking took place.
man is weak and all the good of society derives from the veneration of the
human being.
All English society derives from respect for the individual and his innocence.
A whole massive worldwide empire based on Christ the individual, and his
brothers,
The Sons who came after. "

On Anglesey, in a single plot, there is a stone age burial tomb
A Roman village, with walls and buildings, and a medieval chapel, all of them
deserted and at peace
So, God is in the land, the time and places.

He speaks with life, your place of life, which shelters you
As Chester did, similarly ancient and undefeated by despair.

The proper response in the human mind is hope."

60

We were alone, moving now past life's origins
Into the coldness of empty dead space, mere solids and liquds and meaningless
gases
Which no living thing had ever seen.
Like as they think they will find it,
They who kill themselves
All dead, lifeless, with no responsibility or mind there.
It was evening now. The place was desolate, windy, raining.

"The greatest virtue that the man can cultivate is love.
God is talking to you, by all means.
And when there is nothing here around, no objects, no light
What then? Is it all over, all his care for you?
No, it is not the end.
For, just as I ascended to heaven after my death
I left a space for you, in the emptiness of the tomb
Where my body, my real body had risen and ascended from,
A place for you to fill with your living body."

The place was desolate, but there were two of us, and this was as if the place was
A perfect paradise. For people are the main thing.

"And, notice, the barrenness of the place is like the emptiness of the hermit's
cell.
It's ideal for meeting God.
For my father is not in this world; he gives the world to you.
He is not of it or in it.
And turning from it is necessary, at the highest end.
So that you love the giver, and not his Gifts, so to speak.

The most glorious thing ever made is the organisation of a human society of
Christians, sure. Whether the British Empire; or the Byzantine Empire and
Church; or the Russian attempts recently,

Where Patriarch Kirill and Putin's Russian state brought Orthodoxy back from
the Soviet eclipse.
Countering the collapse of Byzantium, too.

And think of Liverpool, the second richest city in the British Empire, only a
few decades ago,
With its port, and ships and its splendour
Bringing the entire world into one place, under an English rule
Dominated by a Christian idea.
Such a society of order and Christian love is the most perfect thing imaginable."

We did find someone:
"All that is gone. A proud boast, these days, is that Liverpool
Is still the most important town in England and the world
And, not a part of England at all, but the capital city of Wales."

Who was talking?
"Yet, when all that is gone; and it does fall in the end,
Despite defence of the walls as at Byzantium, against the Western knights who
Destroyed the defence and liberty there, more or less by accident,

When all that is gone,
The love of God is still possible in you, and necessary.
There was no instruction from God to build an empire,
Nor to revolt against such a beautiful incredible thing.
But he did instruct us to love God, and love each other."

I think that the one talking was that misguided man, John Lennon,
Whose mother was born around the corner from my home,
And who was shot dead in New York when I was a child.

"You were that rebel against institutions, orders and conventions
And rebel against God. What are you doing here, so high up and remote from
all comfort and other people, on your own?"

"I" he said, "was a singer,
And espoused love like a new religion. The one who said
'I don't believe in Jesus' and a number of other things.
'I just believe in me, my wife and me'.
There was no damage done by this.
I was swept up by forces beyond me
Perhaps my band, The Beatles, were a compensation
For the American public's loss of the President in those times;

The times when the USA was stealing the British Empire and making its own.
Our music a sop. But I died before I could make peace with the world
And tell a more balanced tale of what I believe.
For, I believe in me, and what is the basis of me as a thing
Can only be the higher person of God.
And that, I love, him I love. That, anyway, is what is going on here
While I learn how to love God most. The origin of all things
The draw and root of desire."
My master responded to him, telling him:
"You were trying to fill the void left by my absence, my departure
My ascension. You were protestant, and angry with God.
This was a mistake. But now, learn the truth. Be forgiven."

We left him there. Walking on slowly. Night fell, the end of the sixth day.
We sat down and I lay down to sleep, anxious about what was going to happen next.
And excited, my stomach stirring.

61

"Master," I said, as we lay down, at the end of the world
All life extinct, all light extinguished, at the end of that ceremonial sixth day,
"Tell me about the love of others, your second commandment
Or the second of the two laws in which pair all the laws of God are contained."
He rested his head against a stone, and put part of his coat over the stone as a pillow.

"The church of England died at first slowly, and then very quickly at the end, in a rush to finish.
It lost contact with me. But the English church kept up paying lip service to the law of loving others.
You often heard the Archbishop of Canterbury in the last years, speaking passionately about how love of your neighbour means everything.
Such a theory is no better than suicide. For, one may only love others
In fulfilment of my command, when once you have devoted every ounce of love in your heart to God the Father, and to me, in the love of yourself.
For you are God; and you are God only when you love me. And loving God is the first commandment.
And what that means, is proper worship.
They forgot how to worship, And then
They forgot how to know and love me.

And, when once you love God, you will know how to love others. The Archbishop and his Church, neglecting me, forgetting how to worship, forgot how to love their neighbour."

"But if they did not love you, what did they love?" I asked.
"They loved nothing. They simply used the old buildings and phrases
They had inherited, but failed to suffuse them with meaning.
"It is a risk taken by Erastian churches, those which are very close to the state.
They become urgently interested in the social and human aspects of their organisation.
They engage in covert barratory
They get involved in simony,
Money, commerce, doing the right thing by each other,
Is their highest value. They don't love, however.

So, in order to make people come to church, and be their followers

They began to think and say things, and employ people in positions of power,
who could appeal to the secular interests of the people of England.
They stopped worshiping God, but
To appease the feminists, they made women bishops
To appease the protestors for sexuality, they did not object to homosexuality
Openly to prove that they were like Christ,
They made interventions in policing the borders of the country,
And encouraged foreigners to come and live here.
They got involved in politics
And they were ridiculed.
These things, and others, made the Church unfit.
Christians were no longer being created by their organisation.

The light of truth shows, that the first love is for God, regardless of what people
are doing and thinking. And next, love of yourself, and then, love of your
neighbour and enemies.
We love others, because we see in them the same eternal soul we have first been
so diligent to find and protect.
Similarly, we allow immigrants into the country, if at all
After we have taken especial care of our God, self, and family.
If there is room for immigration, then only then can it be allowed, very
carefully.
Protect the borders of your land with strong military and fierce patriotism
The Church of England forgot even these basic principles.
Letting foreigners, and the wilfully bad and unrepentant
Ruin the country was never a Church's role."
We slept; I slept. For sleep is undesirable, but necessary for the mind
So wearied by learning and shocked by seeing.

62

When morning came, we found ourselves with a bright sunlight
And the sandy rocky ground was not so bad.

The sound of a man approaching, singing:
"Make the ways straight, the kingdom of God is at hand.
Repent"
St John, the Forerunner, the Baptiser it was.
He came out of the desert, one way, and made way for my master
to go back the way he had come
There was a river there, of fresh water

And John sang: "Blessed is he who comes in the name of the Lord".
Now my master approached him,
And he and I were both baptised again, afresh in that water.

From the heavens, a dove descended, and a voice:
"This is my beloved Son, in whom I am well pleased".

Now, Christ was not beside me when I rose from the water and looked around
for him.
St John was still there, but not my master.

"Where did my master go?" I asked. The Forerunner pointed the way that he
had come from
And I went through the water. I imagined that I could see him some distance
away
Heading into the distant wilderness.

But, the Baptiser held me back, holding my arm.
I began to shout after him, and tried to break free of his grip.
He let me go, but also pointed to a figure following my master
A black shade, walking freely behind him, indifferent to his surroundings,
Striding, after him.
"Leave them, Christ, and his enemy, to work it out between them".

And so, I came out of the water on the other side, and afraid,
and therefore relieved not to have to follow Christ on his difficult task in the

desert,
I acceded to St John's request and his company.

63

St John the Forerunner was on his way onward out of judgement,
But he said: "I must wait here, like a sergeant;
I will be last, watching for the last and slowest ones to arrive.
Sit down now, wait until our Lord returns
And that is what we did. Nobody came our way.
It was as if, this wait was mine alone; or, that despite this being a path all had to travel
So that they could have their sins forgiven
I was not going to meet anyone else there.

"This is the last of the Feasts and tests
Each man must undergo, before the last rebirth.
And all will pass through here, after they've seen the other places
But now, this is for you only, it is your judgement."

"How can Christ be all to all men,
And a specific instance also?
How can each person relate all the time to God
And he to them?
Is life like a dream,
In which a world is created
For each individual sleeper?
And yet, how do the sleepers interact
And how can their world be a single world, created once
As well as made for each to live inside?"

It was like this that I framed the question to John for Baptist
As we waited at the last station. And he to me:

"It is God giving his mind or a part of it,
And its abilities, to the man.
Consciousness, heart, and mind, would be what opens the world up to be.
He reconciles the worlds of each man alive in One.
And that is how freedom is possible,
How the distinction of mind from matter is unreal.
The mind comes with the material world, as its servant
And the material world would not exist without mind.

It would allow miracles and intuitions to be possible.
But it would imply that God alone is real
He directs the postal system of things going on.
How could our world really be shared?
It would allow miracles and changes very easily.
It would imply that the world is entirely self contained to you.
It would make God essential.
It would make it impossible for the world to exist unless God
Were overseeing it, dreaming or creating it in every moment.
It would make the point of life this: to get to know God.
But the world would not be real. Yes, but it would be more real
It just wouldn't be 'self subsisting'. It would not be a set of random objects.
It would all mean something.
But wouldn't Christ be multiple?, and the all the worlds be multiple?
Not at all, for words shared between people
And culture and history, are from God, and sustained by him
Just as the present moment is.
Leibniz had the same idea. But he said, the it would be the best of all possible worlds.
I disagree. I think that it implies that we have fallen to disunity and blindness
And that it could be better, and will be so.
And, with this intimate relationship between reality, self and God
We are capable of purifying ourselves from the illusion
And seating ourselves in the place where God is
Becoming godlike. It also permits the existence of angels
Particularly on the individual intimate level."

You will proceed to see what the Resurrection is, and I will wait here, the last of men
And the forerunner!"

I think that this was the final day of my time, but not as the sun and earth collude in normal time.
Each day could last forever, or could be over in no time at all, there.
The Earth's time was still being rolled up and wound down

Back there, it takes 365 days and one quarter, for the Earth to travel one circuit around the sun.
That is, properly the spin of the earth on its own axis, which makes a day,

Happens a bit more than 365 times
for the planet to circle all around the sun, and come back to the same point as it
started at.
Of course, a cycle of the moon around the Earth is 28 days.
And the Moon turns on its axis one full turn ever 28 days, so we see only one
face of it.
And, note this last irony of all space and time
While the Sun is 400 times bigger than the moon
It is also 400 times the distance from the Earth that the Sun is.
"It has a 30 degree tilt, so the Earth's axis is not perpendicular to the plane of its
movement.
But the tilt is not fixed, and sometimes it varies and shifts around. Every 25
thousand years or so, it returns back to its starting point
As regards its dithering wobble of tilt.

But none of this any longer made any difference.
Such are not the means by which time is measured here."

It was around midday on the seventh day when we saw somebody coming,
St John and I arose to meet him
But it was not Christ, as I had expected; they were a couple of figures, holding
hands,
A little girl, skipping along, with her hair in pigtails either side her head,
And a tall thin boy, with the shambling gait of a young man
who has not yet gained full possession of his deportment, and appears to be
embarrassed with his new height and physical strength.
I knew who they were, though I had not seen them for many years
because they had been guarded jealously by their jealous mother
who was confirmed in her decision to be acquisitive by the judiciary and the
state.

I walked to meet the two of them, and picked up my daughter in my arms,
And put my other arm around my son's shoulders.
I kissed them both many times; and became short of breath because of my
emotion.
In my heart, I thanked God many times,
Looking at them and seeing so much happiness all around me.
Finally, I was able to say: "Where is our Lord gone? And how did you get
here?"

"Dad, Jesus, brought us here, last night, or whatever it was.
He came to the house; I don't know if it was a dream, or what.
And he brought us here, walking." Hope, said this.
"Lots of walking. We came quite a long way", the boy said.
"And what happened before you met me here?"
Hope told me: "Well, he told us, that he had remade the world,
And that we should come and see you, and show you the new world.
He said, that we knew much better, or as much about these things
Than you. Especially Jaxon, and you must be our dad again."

"Okay, then, let's go." I said.
I did not mention their mother, and they did not either.

"Why did he need to go into the wilderness again
And confront the devil, the Evil One?" I said.
"Christ is both entirely human in his will, and entirely divine.
So, he is a man. And the devil needs time and opportunity to see
If he can still win – which is possible."

64

My happiness and relief was great, to see my children
And to know, that the Lord had given them to me,
and that nothing at all could take them from me.
No woman, no state, nor my enemies; I could look after them, and know they were safe.
I had no intention of letting them go again,
I did not let go of my girl, nor put her down on the ground
For as long as seemed right to me, to reassure myself.
And I frequently put my arm around the shoulders of my son.
But gradually, I became calm; but I hardly stopped thanking God,
That they were with me, and that they were alive and had seen nothing.

"The first thing to know, dad, is that the festivals of judgement are not yet over.
For now, it is the Feast of the Entry into Jerusalem."

"What can this mean?" I said, I became afraid, but did not let my children see.

"Well, dad, see the waters separate over here, with our path
And see the road ahead, that way is the last city, the Holy city.
It's a dream or a vision of God."

We walked on, and the earth around us was simply misshapen and utterly barren.
There were rocks, and huge shards, and an uneven horizon.
It was as if, and I could not be sure any longer, because my guide was gone,
The earth was itself just being formed.

It was not entirely round, spherical; nor was all of it gathered in one place
Gravity was still sucking in and pushing out,
And, through the dark sky, you could see various foreign bodies in addition to the moon.
But worst of all, the moon was all jagged and misshapen, too.
"How long ago is this, for the planets and the Earth to be unfinished?" I said.
The children told me: "We don't know. How should be know?"

We came across a pathway, and there were other people nearby now. I didn't know who they were, nor did I care to know.

I was anxious to keep the little ones safe and content.

In the distance, some kind of walled city or complex, a place of safety.
And here, on the road, at the sides, people were laying out rushes and palm
leaves..

I realised with alarm the tragic thing which was going to happen.
Was I going to be asked to put palm leaves on the ground?
I knew what would be next. Christ came by
But it was not exactly the man I knew, happily
But one who seemed not to know me.

He rode a donkey, and was acclaimed with the old Hossanah.
The animal he rode was a lovely horse, with old Celtic and Roman crosses on it.
There were many saints around him, of the Isles.
He dismounted, when the horse stumbled
And the saints made way for a Venerable man
Who had the Orthodox Cross with him.

And they led Christ further, over the palms to the sound of their singing.

65

And now, twelve of the saints bearing lion and unicorn arms gather around him
And a table is brought out.
They sit around the table. Here, the Bishop of Rome takes precedence, in the
place of Peter.

And one of them, one of the trusted men led by Peter,
Leaves and Christ announces that he will be betrayed.

Now, they arise, and the table is moved away,
Christ sits alone, and prays with his father
Making the disciples flee.

Now, soldiers arrest and take Christ to the prison.
"Can you see him in the jail, Dad?"
My daughter asks to be put on my shoulders, and other people are watching
this.

In the jail, the Roman Bishop, with the symbolic keys
First betrays him and survives aside from him,
And forms a group of his own followers; his own church.
and then soldiers,
who demand a reason, why they should have a Lord separate from their own
crowd
They remove his robes
They interview him, and chain him, and despise him
Saying that the church doesn't need him.

"Don't let them do this!" I said, but my son reminded me.
"Dad, it's not real; do you think they can crucify him again?"

The skies meanwhile were furry with streaks of coloured plasma
And lights from the swirling gases
And the wandering rocks of one kind or another
from the asteroid belt were sometimes smashing
into the Earth and delivering ice and water
And chunks of gold and other things from distant stars.

"What's it for then?" I said.
"To teach you, I suppose".

He was dressed next in robes for a king
In form of an Englishman. They were English robes
And there were also other prisoners, and soldiers
Who dressed him in their bits and pieces in mockery.

They put a crown on his head, and gave him a sceptre
As if he were a worldly ruler and would do the bidding of the mob.
Finally, these were stripped off him
And he was made naked, while thieves and criminals were allowed to roam freely
While Christ was put in a cell.
Loud voices of angry women were heard.
And people with familiar and foreign voices and faces,
His enemies, were demanding his death

66

After that he was brought out with the Cross to be sacrificed on it.
It was inevitable. "But this is supposed to show you history"
The children said. But I was moved. It really was him, my friend and master.
And so it was that he carried his cross again
There was a steep jagged rock nearby, like those at the top of Cadr Idris
And, it was not so steep that he could not walk up it
Alone and under no compulsion, he went.
But then, the saints who had been at the start, and the others who came after
And some of the men who had been around when the arrests were taking place
Returned.
They were able to help him to make his way.
And they did the work of crucifying him.
"What does it mean" I asked, "That the old saints and the church actively
engage in this?"

"Dad, what else is the sacramental meal, the communion,
Than the eternal recreation of God's sacrifice for us?
It is not cruel. It is a duty."

And so it was. The milky way was spread out, above him
The dark sky with millions of distant stars visible.
And the clouds swirling, at the end of the Earth's life.
The cross was raised.

"This is part of the judgement, and punishment, too"
I said. "Shall we survive without the Earth, and with God?
The earth is moving. The lights are going out."

I saw the lights going out, and was afraid very deeply.
It felt as if the Father himself, the Creator had died.

"I ask you, though, didn't we all die, and didn't all of them disappear?"

"Christ's death is different. It was death where resurrection was intrinsic to the
act.
It was not suicide, because he knew he would arise.
And it was not meaningless perishing and disappearing, as it could be

understood when other men die.

Rather, it is a sacrifice.

The sacrifice is carried out again; allegorically, to demonstrate a historical account.

And, really, because you have known him – he was a man, so this is a truthful account.

And as God, showing his love – so as God's sign of love for us, theologically.

And as literature, so you may read it as a story.

The theological aspect is the highest way in which this event is understood

Because it demonstrates God's nature to us

Not as a Father, because the Father did not die;

But as love itself, so that the very nature of all reality is

That we learn the meaning of all things as God loving us

And that we must above all and first recognise and submit to being loved with our own care for God."

67

And, doing so, he suffered as any man would suffer, no different
He has a man's will, and a man's body
He was afraid, he could have backed out of it.

He was injured, and his hand was nailed to the cross.
The other hand was pulled tight to the other side, and nailed also.
His foot and then the other foot were injured cruelly,
And he was in pain for many hours, afraid, and humiliated,
His arms hurt him, and his back was arched because he could not stand
properly.
His head was weighed down; he sweated and groaned.
That strong body and capacious intellect was tortured.

We stood around for many hours, and sat down, waiting for a happy end.
Christ died, of course. My friend, my master, alone.
I was weeping, to myself, and did not let my children see.

And, he was brought down to the ground again, having been punished
In this way, by some obscure people, almost secretly.

I know these details because I had moved close to the place where my master
was,
And I heard him cry out at the end, and saw that he was dead.
And saw that he died alone. When that happened,
The Earth breathed its last also
And we drifted out of the orbit of the sun.
So everything went dark. The sky was bright only by the large number of stars
Which were very clear and more numerous than in previous times.
Our bodies became lighter, and ready to float into the air.

But the women were at work binding his body and they carried it to a grave
And laid it to rest.
There, his mother, the Theotokos, desolate for the loss of her own meaning,
her reason for being, crouched over his body.
And in the vast empty cave of being the body went.
We were stood,
Or consumed also. Surely, we were imagining our bodies and the place

Because there was no more time or space.

Then, the process of world exhaustion set in, and the world as a whole simply gave up,
And rolled backward at immense speed
So that all the parts were sucked up, through space toward a central point;
As into a black hole, where gravity even consumes all light.
All that was left was, a single point of light.

All the millions upon millions of stars which had been hung on the sky,
So many decorations for the night sky of mankind, and God's Son,
All the elements, planets, dust and gas, every atom of them were gone.

My children and I sang or spoke: "O mother of God, cry for us also
And ask your son to come back. We need help.
We are neither alive nor dead, and we have no world.
Mother of God, pray for the resurrection of your Son
And ask him to help us."

My children and I held each other,
And it was dark, but I reassured them that it was going to work out.
I also thought of my distant wife
And my hopes for life in future times,
And I do not remember anything of what happened next.

RESURRECTION

68

I am the son of God, not in the lineage of Adam.
I found this out when I was awoken by my children.
I was rebuilt, put back together
And in need of a world.

I had not seen my children for three years before the final end.
I explained to them: "I never gave up hope that you would come and see me one day.
I imagined that some unexpected event would come along to push you toward me.
But I always feared, the heartless state would keep you
Away from me, and make you one of theirs in their terrible care,
instead of me and my care, your father."
"We know, dad. We already know" they said,
But I went on:
"Why didn't I come and see you before? Because
The people of those degenerate times would have been involved straightaway
And removed me from our union.
The state has become an agent, like a king. With properties, powers, and agents.
And they paid your mum, like a husband. She was unable to divorce herself from them.
And I was not welcome, and not treated like a man.
So, I had no choice but to stay away."
And they said nothing but smiled, as if it did not matter:
But I said: "I was always worried about you, in the world as it was
Unfit to live in. You were not going to school
And there were many people around who were bad and abusive to children.
Children can't defend themselves, and they need a father.
The state had set about to destroy the family and fathers,
Destroying mothers was harder and they still existed, when it all ended."

Again, my daughter held on to me, and I picked her up.
My son stood watching me.

They say, "You are dead, dad."
And I: "Are we dead? Is it possible?
And why are you two happy and so confident? "

"We have been in heaven for a long time now, or, we came straight here
Because children who died came straight here, no witness of the destruction or judgement.
We learn about the world in its heavenly state, those few who saw the end of the world.
So, we see everything. Within God are all things, all the creation.
I can see within God all things. All the ways that things link together, and all the lives
And experiences of others. So there is nothing I don't know about you."

"Will I have the same vision of God", I asked.
"You will have to progress slowly in education. To see how the paradise is made
And then at the summit, look directly at God, as we do."
So, I was created or born a second time. And I was not alone, because everyone
who had got on the great race from the nuclear start, and through all the destruction
Was here, too.

Christ had already created my world
And given me his consciousness. That is the creation of man.

So we set off. "So that this is a real life and that we are safe here
Lord, have mercy on us" they said. And they went on singing.
My son first, and the little one following:
"For peace and salvation of our souls, Lord have mercy".

There were only the things of the mind, I suppose. Images, memories, the sounds
Were not present in time and place; now I look back and think that that was not possible.

"For every city and people, Lord have mercy"
And yet we were travelling somewhere.

"Dad, the whole vision of God will be revealed, gradually.
First, at the start, the old masters of the old world
Are at the entrance, servants, like deacons in a church
Going out to gather in the people."

Isaac Newton, the master and most powerful mind of the West, who
Disclosed all the laws of matter,
He put me before the screen of the new world
An unmoving barrier between God and us, which is our senses
He was here.

In heaven, I found myself with senses of sight, and taste and touch, and so on
And therefore, of space and time. It was a great screen and barrier
between me and God, in front of the eternity and power of God.
Newton, the Englishman, he took me to the screen.
And Gottfried Leibniz, his European equal,
I saw them there, just like their companion, St Maximos the Confessor,
The greatest mind of the East, and founder of the monastic orders
Where the spirit was most well known, calling together all Platonism, and
Christ's followers.

And so, with the world open, and I was through the door to the world.
I went back to the new world
With my children.

69

What did I see around me, through the door of the screen
Of the world and this new existence?
It was still a place where there were people; only people
Just as you don't notice the details of your environment in dream or even in life
Just the things you need to see. And I could only see people
My dear children, the German philosopher,
The knight of science from England, and the saint of theology
Out of Byzantium. The philosopher, said:
"Bless this existence, this man, a window onto the world
Who is able to see God, he should be a temple,
A site of vision of God, and worship".

And there were two other men, there. They brought me to the screen again,
And said: "So is man created."
And then the two of them were beside me
"These are the philosophers Charles Darwin from Shropshire,
Who went to the far ends of the Earth over many years in that famous ship.
And unlocked some of the mysterious doors of existence."
That's what my daughter said and the other joined in:

"Don't think, that you are a fool, now, pushed about by saints, instructed by scientists
Led around by your own children, as the daughters of Oedipus
led the blind man around in heroic bronze age Greece.
You've got to be given a body, which makes you stupid and corporeal,
Except that you'll also be conscious of what God intends in full,
You won't be pushed around by your own skin and bone and fat and pleasure.
God put the five of us, here. I'm St Gregory, the monastic founder in the West.
And for what it is worth, you have the potential
To know and see clearly just as St Maximos, and I,
And Darwin, Newton and Gottfried Leibniz do."

"Life was an ailment before. And vision was cloudy.
Only by looking to God, could you see what things meant.
Now, you can see Him in things, and existence
Is not the place of sweat and hunger it was."

It was Darwin, then, who brought me by the hand to a woman
Stood to one side; It was my wife, Galya.
"They used to say, that angels are without sex.
But this is not so for human beings.
A woman is a person who can bear and nurture children
With whom a man should live,
God's love makes a hierarchy of delegated duties and affections
From God, to man, and from man to woman, and children,
And from this the various Ranks of society and order
In which each has his place
In the care for the earth and for other people.
The poor, the strong, the weak, and the responsible
The neighbour
Each has a place and a role in the delegation of love and care
And the exercise of keeping what is right."

In affection for her and gratitude for her safety,
My heart opened and I embraced her.

"Now where is my first wife," I said;
"After my reflection on the matter at length,
I am ashamed, that I made the mistake of marrying badly that woman.
But where is she? Don't my children, need their mother."

"Her fate is not here or there. Some people simply did not make it.
And we leave that out of the consideration.
But neither is your second wife yours.
Each has its own world, each person is going about his own business.
And, when you are remade completely, soon, Galya can be with you again.
But in the meantime, we will move on".

I felt her body in my arms for the second time since the end of the world.
Then, my children moved me away from the five deacons and servants of God
And from her.
And just as an explosion, so useful for mining the earth when it cracks rock
open,
Can be brought about by joining two compounds which react to one another
And cause energy to be released very quickly,
Or just as the explosion of a gun starts a race, so we were off

And went our separate ways for the second time.
An explosion is due to any chemical reaction or mixing of compounds
Which bond with each other, and in doing so are
Sucking up or releasing energy, slowly or quickly.
And you may initiate any reaction
by introduction of some fire or spark.
Then, when the reaction takes hold, it releases all the energy.
So, released energy can make an explosive if the it is released all at once
Rather than slowly. It is not the amount, but the speed of the energy release.
Take gunpowder, a compound of two types of substance.
Introduce a spark, which consumes the substance in a small part
And the small part's demise releases energy, heat and sparks
Which consumes all the rest of the substance which has been gathered.
A chain reaction as the sparks from the first fire contaminate the next,
With huge amounts of fire and heat from a small amount of substance.

70

"Bless the Lord, O my soul", were words I could hear being sung from
somewhere,
But there was also some words from my son.
"Slow burning fuels are better for controlled chemical reactions;
Coal, mined from the ground, can be dried out by being heated
And then turned into coke. Burning dried coal, coke or charcoal,
The temperature of the fire is greater.
You need higher temperature fire, if you want to get metals from rocks,
The rocks with metals inside are called ores.
You'll need to melt the metals which are inside the rocks, so the metals drip out.
For this, you need a hot fire.
A hut or little house for the fire is needed, a kiln
And a means of shooting air at the fire.
Hot fire needs lots of oxygen and air because the fire feeds of the air. "

"Do we still need to know these things, and to work, here?"
I asked my daughter.
"Let yourself be instructed now, by the men who know what the future will be.
Works and also social matters have to be relearned," my son said.

"No man knows everything about the proper order of things.
Opinions vary, and no opinion can be proven to be absolute. People fight.
So, Locke had it, that tolerance is the great public virtue.
Let people disagree, but tolerate each other.
Let the old proven ways remain.
And, so it is in heaven."
"Who is he, talking?" I said to my son. "Who are you?"
"I am here, to bring to your mind, before you enter the physical real world,
The underlying order, the logos, the conceptual mind of God
Which you inherit. I am William of Orange, but don't take only my word for it,
the word of God's Englishman. But also see St Ambrose,
Bishop of Milan, who first made the churchman
the equal and the superior of the temporal emperor."

And I saw, or somehow received, a new mind
By vision, or gift, the conceptual essence, the meaning of all reality
In so far as the individual, God, others, and the world, all form a harmony.

"That William, who pursued the King, James Second,
Because that Stuart could not tolerate the English as they were,
but preferred the Catholics and his friends.
No way to run a state, in hatred of the land and people."
"This is true."
And Ambrose spoke: "But a state is not run for men's good only,
But so that the people can know God.
And it is so, that a ruler and a commonwealth of people in a social contract
Need a ruler who bows to God.
If any sense is to be made of human life at all, then God's needs, which are in us,
As aspiration to heaven, and intellectual understanding
Will be heard. But neither should the head of a Church
Demand things of the state's ruler."

"The body is to be put aside, in favour of the spirit.
Homosexuality, or gratuitous sex, is forbidden;
And Hope sang: "Bless the Lord, blessed art thou, O Lord",
With the accompaniment of a vast number of voices,
and the movement of things, and the appearance,
from in front of the screen of all senses, the world.
"Now that the principles of the world are understood,
The world can appear!" said Jaxon.

71

The curtain of the real world is drawn
"Help us, save us, have mercy on us, and keep us, O God",
These were words from the liturgy of the church which were being repeated
And my son smiled at me, and took the three of us through the world
Now fully formed. To the great gatekeepers of reality and how men interact
Namely with their language;
For concepts are silent and laws aren't practical
Until they become human. And the poets make them human.
"Here at the entrance to reality, father, a couple of men you know,
Or whose books you knew well
That tragic and cynical man who died writing his Don Juan,
Involved in liberating Greece from the Ottomans.
This liberation of the Orthodox lands, finally achieved with the Royal Navy,
Was helped by the petition and example of this lord and poet."

"Died in his late thirties, in Greece; or, escaped from England, more like.
Hypocritical people, island race, no place to be alone.
And what poet has not had to escape his shameful mistakes?" my son said.
And then to him: "What do you make of the Orthodox conflict with the West
today?
They are trying to dominate the Orthodox and Christian land of Russia, the
Third Rome."
"That's in the past now," he said. "Would I have escaped
To Russia, and seen action in Ukraine?
Possibly, if I were alive in the end of days.
In this instance, the Russians are the Orthodox and the cultured
Fighting for freedom, against the domination of the rest of Europe and the
West.
The world complained, that they were violent.
There is always violence at the origin of a nation,
And when it is threatened throughout its time."

He looked around, and pointed out to me the place where we were.
It was the landscape of the sea coast, I do not know if Misolonghi,
Or North Wales –places of freedom and beauty without comparison,
His and mine. There were terns nesting or breeding,
Making their racket, and somewhere out there I expect

To find the bottlenosed dolphins and the seals of the northern seas.
"Are there things to do, in heaven?"
I asked him. "What did you expect?" he said.
"The boredom and the constriction of the heaven
Of the Protestant clerics; all that restraint and terror?
No, there is a great deal to learn, more so
Than in the other life."

"Are we going to stay here for a while?" I asked the children.
"Where are we going next? Do we ever sleep?
I'm tired, and have learned and exhausted myself."
"Not yet, dad. See, there are other people coming behind us, and see inland,
The shapes of places where people live.
Before sleep, for human beings are not infinite in their capacities,
Notice we are welcomed by other liberators
From the soil and the sweat of the life on Earth
Like Abraham Lincoln over there".
There was a house sat above some land which went down to the sea's edge,
And it was the old American president up there, the one
Who put an end with clemency to an outrageous civil war.
There were others, too, who had done their best
In crippling and stupid wars of that kind,
As when the Western knights came to Byzantium and ruined it,
But some of them were men who could rise above this kind of ruin,
And were fit for heaven.

72

Likewise, another poet I saw there,
Who came home from India, to Sussex, on the coast.
Rudyard Kipling, one of those on that coast,
Came out to meet me as we came to a sort of garden
Running down from a great house on a headland.
My children said to me: "Let this man show you how God has made home,
Even here, after life and death."
"We would beg God to give us those things
Which we want most in our hearts.
We are glorified by divine kindness and not forsaken.
A man needs a place to live and to rest and sleep in the night;
In some blessed ignorance. The whole vision of God is too much for most of us.
It is better, to be able to praise and implore, and ask for kindness from Him
Than to burn in the direct light.
So, it is the case, that he made the heaven
So that a man can have some property and land. "
"Did anyone see the Father make the Earth again?" I asked him.
"It's not the Earth, and it was not the Father
Who made or remade creation.
It is understood to have been the work of the Son.
If anyone saw, then I wasn't one of them.
I remember waking, after my death in England of old age,
Disappointed with England, and mourning my son.
I died, but was awakened in the final conflagration.
I did want to stop the march onward,
But stubbornly followed where I was being led.
Besides, interested to know the future.
When the final judgement was made, and darkness fell,
I found myself here, on the coast. With my son.
And it is enough for me; I'll go on further inland one of these days.
Meantime, I do pray unceasingly, quietly,
in happiness and confidence I felt once in the British,
but which I now feel in God alone, and in all."

We walked further, investigating this idea,
That there is a place of home in heaven,
Like those many mansions Christ spoke of once,

According to St John.

There was a man, we met as the lights went dim for evening
Who explained British history to me and my children.
After we left the Kipling hill station,
We were walking hand in hand, my daughter and me on the sand and shingle.
Wales, or Scotland, or Ireland, or England,
One of the beaches there. He said:
"These places, these distinct cultures and places,
Geographically different, and racially,
Are and were joined into a small empire in itself;
And being seafaring, and an island, very confined,
The people are forced to learn to work in harmony and trust."
"Who are you?" I asked him, and walked toward him.
He was outside in the garden, behind his fence, doing work.
"I am that Loyola that brought strength
Back to the Catholic branch of the church
After the disastrous attacks of the north.
See, there was no headway of my organisation,
A saintly fighting organisation, except in Ireland.
The English reformed church, especially after the Popes grew afraid of my
Jesuits,
Organised and motivated like the Jesuits
Went out to the Americas, the Caribbean,
Canada, and India, the Australasian islands,
And starting at the south, and extreme north of Africa in Egypt,
To capture most of the world's people.
Including the middle east and also China and Tibet.
It was a triumph of a unified mankind,
But with one fatal flaw: it lacked true immovable religion.
So, even at the moment of absolute divine accomplishment,
When the British army liberated Jerusalem,
At that time, the men involved were without faith,
Or religious guidance. They have started to believe
Those things which made their empire of power,
Reason and peace, liable to fall."

"Sir, I am looking for a place for my family,
My children to stay the night. How did you find somewhere here?"

He replied. "We're all new here.
I contemplate with my God, and see him always, so
I was happy to have a hut by the sea, like St Ninian in Galloway,
Or like the hermit's chapel after St Gobain or Gawain in Pembroke.
But the first night I was here, I was put here by the angel of this place,
To meet people like you.
I have no doubt, that if you continue along,
you will find somewhere to stay.
On earth, in our first life, we had to struggle to get property.
And, unless you own anything of your own,
How to understand the law and nine tenths of the law
Concerned with the protection of property?
Children love the sea and the seaside.
Go along, and God will provide."
So he spoke, and we left.

73

And so it was, I provided a place for my daughter and my son
In an old deserted church at the sea's edge, where
Comfort and food had been left for us.
But I did not have any rest, while I was learning. They say, that sleep deprivation
Helps to make people stop thinking, and to submit
And I do not think that God or his agents intended this. But so it was.

There was the recent saint
Cardinal Newman. We discussed, as if I were sat at the table,
The laws on property:

"English process, for dispute resolution, tends to look on both parties as rivals,
And the court tries to make them come to a bargain,
award something half way between the two
Based on the arguments they make. So, if you argue badly, you get little.
This has led to the profession of pleaders in court,
who know what arguments to make.
But at least, the judges are independent in their decisions.
Only the laws they must follow are issued by Parliament.
Judges make up their own minds in the court room.
And also precedent, which is common law – that can be called on
Regardless of parliament.
When a judgement has been given long ago,
When a law seems right and is followed by nature of right and wrong
And it derives from our natural Christian instincts
Then it has power over judges, it is the law
Despite what Parliament, or protest or idealists will try to force on the people.
It is inherited and must be accepted with care.
So, the right to self-defence is always protected and right
Even when the Parliament and its police attempt to make it contrary to law
And say: 'You can't be violent at any time for any reason'. Such things
Are contrary to the law of the land for ever.
The English, they're allowed to do whatever
Is not explicitly prohibited by statute, or
What does not obviously deny the common law of England.
And, the state oversees the courts, but does not own them.

In England, the state itself is just a pleader,
One side, and can be prosecuted."
So spoke that English cardinal.

"Across the water, in France, all is different,
The state provides the judges, and their job is to find the truth.
They determine sentences on the facts and logic alone.
As in England, a man is judged not by the state, but by his peers, his equals.
But in France, you may only do, what is explicitly stated in the code, that you
are allowed to do.
These interesting questions fill up your dreams.
But, like the Constitution of the USA,
These processes do rely on the participants being familiar
With right and wrong, good and bad, as taught by their the church.
It is true, the founding fathers of America
Like those of the French Republic
Were neither Catholic nor Orthodox Christians;
But they were nonetheless, inheritors of the wealth of those Churches.
When the Church fails, the law and constitution withers.
The Christians who died in 1914 in Europe,
Were the last generation who could live
Under those conditions, as a whole generation,
Of shared belief."

And I replied, in the dream: "Their agents, were the police.
Enemies of the people in France.
Hopeless at the end, in England,
Where they were unable to capture criminals,
but rather, got involved in the pretence of kindness.
The Police Force of Dyfed Powys killed my friend, Spencer.
The policeman, and the law are essential in heaven as anywhere else.
But what is heaven" I asked, "if it is so like the old Earth?"
"Ah, heaven is the old word. It is the second creation,
Repaired, so that man does not die, and so that he is remade in God's image:
Free, human, and knowing his Father, so never ignoring the law
With clear eyed vision. That is where you are now."

74

When we awoke, my children
Were anxious to go inland,
And find out this world's contents.
And there would be land, hills, valleys, lakes and rivers,
And seasons. In that first hour,
My children made their prayer to God:
"Who hast promised that when two or three are agreed in Thy name,
Thou wouldst grant their requests:
Do Thou Thyself now fulfil the requests
Of Thy servants to their profit,
Granting us in this present age the knowledge of Thy truth,
And in that to come, life everlasting"

"Where exactly are we, do you think?" I asked my son.
"I think we are in Wales, dad."
"What, you think that God has made the world
Geographically the same as it was in the twenty first century?"

We started walking and turned inland
Away from the coast a bit, but reluctant to leave,
And determined never to do so altogether.
"Do you know, we could do with a motor,
Or electricity for some kind of vehicle," I said.
"You need to make the motor carefully,
And refine its production to make it efficient.
But you need a fixed magnet pair;
And a rotating block of metal, though pieces
Or slivers of metal are better,
With insulated copper wire wrapped around and around it.
If you put the rotating copper coil inside the two fixed magnets,
So it can rotate, but not touch the magnets,
And turning the copper rotator requires some effort to overcome their fields,
And then you make the rotator go around that armature.
Then electric charge will start to move inside the copper wire.
With bushes, or little bits touching the end of the copper,
You can tap the electron charge off, and it will flow out like water,
Use the organised moving charge to do electrical things.

The bushes need to touch the copper ends briefly,
So that as the rotator moves, it turns over and switches sides.
Or, if you put electrical charge into the copper coil, it will move and turn over.
Attach a drive wheel to the coil's central rod,
And you have the means of an electric vehicle.
That's what we could do with."

"Dad, we like to walk.
God has given life to the towns and cities, and the people
Of land, courts, and church. We'll see them on foot.

Now, we might see seals or porpoises, little dolphins,
Or fish, and crustaceans, here, on this new ancient coast.
And inland mammals, too; the domesticated cows,
And hedgerow and town animals, like hedgehogs, and foxes
And birds of prey such as hawks and owls, as well as the scavengers like
seagulls,
The intelligent large black corvids,
And singing birds.
They are all around. Badgers too."

"If we are sure that we are in Wales, then we must be north,
Because the sun rises from the right, as we look at the sea.
Then, it stays rather, behind us.
And it is spring, I think. Because the sun does not reach the centre of the sky,
And the temperature is rather colder than it usually is
When the sun reaches these heights in autumn, in my memory."
"So, if we go east toward the rising sun's origin,
Along the coast, we will come to the Dee Estuary,
And find our way home," my daughter said.
We made a litany of all the places we missed, and the people and organisations
"I liked school, sometimes, and my friends", she said.

While we were walking, there was a man at the side of the path, alone
And further along, a few more men.
The first man stopped me; he knew me, he said
Because every man knows by seeing God, or glimpses of God
What God also sees and knows. But I myself had not that power.
"I am that Holderlin who you studied so much, and I know you."

"Strange to meet you here," I said. "How the revived are alive all today.
But, because we do not die, then it makes sense.
Why are you in Wales, and not in your native place, in Freiburg,
or wherever it was you were at home?"

"It is possible to be in two places at once,
of course, when there is no time.
Where there is no time, there is no limitation on being everywhere.
it is possible to travel, at the same instant.
But we should not do that, but enjoy the limitations
permitted us by God, to enjoy our singleness, and personal destiny.
The work of death is finished. The society,
which seemed to me possible on Earth, was not.
But is now. I came hoping only to meet you,
and meet everyone who comes along,
to know all the people in this new city of God."
"Do you know, sir," I asked him, "where our home is
And if we will find it in the same place we left it
When we get there? You, in your discussion of Holderlin
Taught me the value in philosophy of the particular place
For which I am grateful." He told us where.

75

Now as we made our way along the north coast
We came to St Beuno's church at Clynnog-fawr
And the old well, flowing properly now
On the way to Caernarvon, on the pilgrims' path,
And my children were singing,
"In Thy Kingdom remember us, O Lord,"
And we were at the church, overlooking the sea
And, from behind the screen of reality, as it were, came the saints themselves,
To greet us: St Beuno, and also the young woman who was beheaded at Holywell
St Winifred. These were Christians from the old time
Of Alfred the Great, and the formation of the Christian people.
You could include St Bede, Venerable, and St Cuthbert,
Whose relics are in Durham Cathedral.
The cathedrals, and churches, we noticed, were still there
Eternal buildings. But they did not speak to us,
But processed out, and brought the book of the Gospels
As if the book was the person of God, the voice of our great leaders and
forerunners.

And more converts to Catholicism, reviving
What the Revolutionaries in France had almost destroyed,
And the English had destroyed in the time of Henry VIIIth.
GK Chesterton was there, that journalist and convert to the true faith
In a Western guise. A fattish man, like his Father Brown,
He watched the procession with us, the saints all in Green,
With gold braid and the priest had a disk with Christ's face
Depicted on it, on his back.

"During Henry's time, the new church was founded, of course.
With Cranmer's prayer book, and the Protestant martyrs Nicholas Ridley,
And Hugh Lattimore were active.
When his daughter came, she murdered hundreds of them.
And she it was, who by killing all those new English reformers,
Really set the English church apart, and made it resolute."
Out following the Gospel, where three hundred or more men and women,
Who had been burned and tortured and beheaded by the Queen

Daughter of Anne Boleyn.

There was no chance of making England part of Christendom after that.
The religion, cut free from its roots, in the Middle East, withered.

"The more recent inroad of Orthodoxy
From Greece and Russia alone could solve this problem."
"I was Orthodox"
"You still are," Chesterton said.
"Get back to Chester as soon as you can now, you and your dear ones.
And see St Nicholas of Japan,
And St Elizabeth the New Martyr, of the Romanov royal family.
All of those saints and martyrs; you will find them there.
The Tsar, and his family, Christian always,
Praying daily in captivity, and mercilessly slaughtered
With pistols, first the Czar himself, while shielding his children.
Then, the children and his wife were stabbed, and their heads bashed in
By the atheists.
So rulers of Christian lands were ruined. But that is all in the past.
Only the holiness remains."
He meant, go to our old church in Chester and Birkenhead,
To the places where we were introduced
To a true worship of Christ, which had a future
And true guidance.

76

In some respect, the Soviets, and the French revolutionaries,
And the Civil service of Britain,
Had taken over from the representatives of God,
And also usurped the Crown.
But the Crown is no more holy, in most times, my boy said to me:
"The saints of these isles had gone back
To the higher place where they come from.
And note, that the Crown, like the empire under which Jesus was alive first,
Persecuted the people, if they do not worship at the shrine of the state.
In some times, it is not possible to say, in public:
"O come, let us worship and fall down before Christ, O Son of God."
This is why, a society must have both a church,
And a state to do secular activity such as organise property,
But, it should face its subjects as people who are entirely innocent of any crime
This forbids any arbitrary imprisonment.
The innocence of a Christian before the state, as a principle,
Is the highest achievement of any state,
And is retained in heaven."

"And the army is never used in the country, either.
Is there any need for any army in this era, I wonder?" I said to him.

And now, as night began to fall, we lit a fire on the side of the sea
It was warm, and we had a visitor. From out of the screen, the rood screen, you could say
Of reality, behind which the activity of God was going on.
"Where are you going, you three? Do you know?
You are going to the higher mysteries and great knowledge."
I asked, "Who are you?"
"I am from that place where the Christian and the secular were worked out,
According to Roman law, in the code of Justinian.
And I was the Patriarch of that place for a while,
Frequently in exile from the secular authority.
St John the golden mouthed. You have seen,
That the highest reality also recognises the achievements
Of the British in the running of the state.
Creation of parliament, opposing sides,

In place of a king's direct power.
Consisting of land owners on one side,
And business men on the other.
The land owning side will include the princes of the church.
Things will stay the same".
"I have some questions," I said to him,
"Will you sit down with us? Firstly, tell me why so many saints
And philosophers have been here, on our way.
I am overwhelmed." And he:
"Don't think, that in eternity
That it all happened just a few days ago that we were here.
You have your sense of time. And I have mine.
And it flatters you to think, with your mind still in the old way,
That time is limited, and people are busy about important things.
I am here to see you, and saw you from afar, with your children
Where they set up their own shrine in the upstairs room when
The little one was barely able to understand anything except love
And enthusiasm and fun. How many millions of years have I been here
And will be? I have time for you."

"I thank you for that, Father. If there's no passage of time; and the church runs things;
How shall any disagreement be possible? I mean, why is a Parliament valuable?
And, if everyone knows God and his will, then…"

"The real reason why a parliament is needed is, that
The human being can develop higher, and God, too.
But, there need be no war or disobedience of nature
And time will pass – and perhaps there will be another higher rebirth
As God unfolds there, too! So, men do debate
In the darkness afforded us by our Lord.
A space for opposition and policy.
These things are concealed in the greatness of God. "

And I said:
"Do you mean, that we have a task of working and building
And taking up the task of venturing into new worlds
And debating the how and the why?"
He affirmed this.

The sky was without stars at that time
The saint blessed us, and left.
We lay down on the sand, and the breeze, to rest.

77

But the outdoors was a great cathedral itself
And it is as if the great cathedrals of the North, with their gloom and shafts of light
Are the forests where there is natural holiness, and the light comes through the trees
So, the canopy of the trees is the interior of the great cathedral
Besides, in the sky of the renewed earth, it is possible to hear the seraphim singing
"Holy God! Holy Mighty!
Holy Immortal! Have mercy on us"
And we knew that God is love, and was watching us for that evening.

In the morning, we continued,
But Hope wanted water: "Dad I want a drink".
But there are all kinds of holy wells and springs along the coast
And while we were there, sat around the well, Jaxon my son had the idea of calling on some particular saint.
He did so, calling on his favourite, St Paul, the apostle.
I suppose that there is some kind of bush telegram, because within a few minutes, he came to see us.

"The journey you make it not really across a physical geometry or landscape
But within. The Earth now is as it always has been,
The basis, the substrate.
You may be heading home, after having landed on the little isle of Bardsey, near St Mary's well,
But, it is the development of ideas and institutions and virtues which develop in you, not the distance of miles, or sightseeing."
"What, are we becoming?" I said.
"Children of God," was the reply.

He made a fuss of my son, and spoke at length with him.
And they discussed the Philokalia, and its translator and editor, Archbishop Kalistos Ware.
And the original editors and compilers, St Nikodemos and Makarios.

"Sir, do you think, that I could ask to speak with one of them?", my son said.

"What do you want to talk about with those two?" answered Paul,
Don't think that people just turn up at your request!
I am here, and I can be your guide."
The apostle smiled.
"Nikodemos was the scholar
And Makarios was the powerful man of action,
Who stirred up trouble and reasserted Greek national identity.
Isn't that right? Now, their famous work is to do with
The dual nature of man, as an intense spiritual being,
Who needs to practice monastic confinement if he is to know God in person.
And they were specially interested in the physical mental rituals
Which speed your progress toward participation in God.
The breathing exercises, and the repetition of a prayer,
And the self-observation
Until consciousness takes flight,
From the physical body and any particular time and space,
In favour of God's experience and mind.
But they were also aware of the daily life of a monastery.
And the practice of a simple regime,
And, above all perhaps aware of
How the world is so hard to overcome
It is a saint's military warfare."

78

"Sir, why don't we need to eat" I said.
"You can eat. But it is more of a custom for humans, than a necessity now.
Your body does not die, nor suffer from lack of nourishment.
Where there are people, in a society,
And they want to cultivate the land, and then eat as they once did,
Then they can do so."

And that was how St Paul spoke to us. We walked together.
"Are you going to come with us towards Chester?" my son said.
He agreed to walk a part of the way.

"What is fire? Some people have equated fire and the holy spirit,
As Holderlin did, and Heidegger wrote of that," my son was asking this question
Thinking of the mystery of it, how it is not exactly a thing,
"It is the oxygen of the air, becoming hot enough,
That it binds with the carbon of the fuel
And makes a new gas. The formation of carbon dioxide
During this forced mixing of gases,
Takes the form of heat and light;
The air catches fire, so to speak.
We see the same, when we see shooting stars, pieces of rock.
Their speed creates heat, which ignites the air
So they look like stars, but moving quickly and falling.
You can prove that the oxygen is binding with Carbon,
Thus causing the light and the heat
Because if you remove the oxygen supply, the fire goes out.
The heat may continue for a while,
But the chain reaction is put out of action, and cooling begins.
The process, once started, is hard to stop.
Because it perpetuates itself, with the binding of carbon and oxygen
Producing yet more heat.
But you need an initial spark, to set the process going."

"I don't know if you could say, that the holy spirit is like fire" my son said.
"They said, that at Pentecost, the day when the church was founded,
There was a burning and tongues of flame.

And fire like spirit does burn away the merely body, the mere carbon
And it can spread, and communicate.
It is the warmth of God, his guidance, up and away from the mere world.
Or like the gases mixing once ignited
So man and God mix."

St Paul and he spoke, until it seemed to me,
That my son didn't want to take any more of his time.
"Will I be able to talk with you in future?" he asked him.
"In the meantime, I am asking the Orthodox Dostoevsky, to see you.
And you can discuss things with him; the most humble of men,
you will feel no embarrassment in taking up his time."

St Paul had read his mind, and knew what was going on.
Now Dostoevsky did come with us.
But I was amazed, and, I was embarrassed
Because of how my son was ordering them about.
"I just don't understand. Why would you, sir,
The greatest of novelists, come to see us, and here
In this, far Western part of Europe, most rural part of the world.
I would say, that my son is behaving like a child outside a sweetshop
Pressing his nose on the window, and desiring the things inside.
But everyone is obliging him, and coming here.
Further, how is it possible to hear him,
And finally, to arrive here so soon?"

"The child is learning, and that is important.
And I hear him, because prayers are heard by God,
And God can speak with us.
In answer to your final question, time is not what it was
The day, time, space, these in eternity
Are kindly limitations we gladly accept but can overcome.
They are kindly limits, to provide comfort to the human personality and
character
Which needs something fixed and steady.
Coming here is no problem to me at all."

The two of them talked about the seven councils.
Where they established the creed, relating to the Father,

Son and Holy Spirit, and then when heresies
And logical questions about the trinity came to people's minds,
How they resolved these quarrels.
Does the Son have a human nature or a divine one?
Is he human entirely, and only God at his resurrection?
If he is both human and divine, how can he have a single will,
A single vision of reality? Does he have two desires and wills?
And does the Holy Spirit derive from the Son as well as the Father?
The novelist, who wanted Russia to revive Christianity,
And then spread it to the world, enjoyed these historical questions,
And the discussion of the people who had been at the councils.

79

"It had been possible to be in heaven, as we are today, by process of
monasticism
In the old days. But it had not been possible for more than one man at a time to
realise it.
Effectively, I think this is what has been done to this world where we are now.
It is now possible for all people to see what the saint sees, without any special
discipline or effort."
So, the writer spoke
It has been the era of the individual alone,
Overwhelmed by a highly advance state organisation,
Which was very capable of wiping out all individuality and religious linkage to
God.
That is what was happening all over the West,
Where the state had become powerful.
And the writer had recorded it happening in the East of Europe, too.
You see this noticed by George Orwell in his last book quite clearly, too.

We were at the sea's edge.
At the Dee Estuary, at last.

A new man joined us. The former prisoner of Stalin's time
And exile in the USA, Solzhenitsyn.
"You know, the Romans sailed ships up to Chester's Watergate street?
And sailing and trade are essential to the world which is now created by the
Father."
"How can this be?" I asked, "that the activities of commerce
Can continue, when there is already plenty
and men cannot go hungry, and don't argue over power anymore?"

"Ah, but we don't see even now half of God's intentions, or his power.
He has recreated us in Eden. But the future, who knows that?
This attitude was once called Hope."
We heard words in the air, sung:
"Glory to Thee, O Lord, glory to Thee."

A procession was coming along the shore,
And again, saints and various types

Of the new order, those, can we say, who had known theosis
Or Godly presence in life, and knew that its fire
Had purified them of the waste and illusion.

They came out bearing the book of the Gospels, and read it out.
But, it was a ceremony for tradition now, of sweet happiness
Because what Christ had promised
And what had been written down in those books
Had happened.
I held my daughter tightly, to let her see
What I could see.

80

It would be an awfully long way by foot, to the Mersey estuary,
At the top of the Wirral peninsula at Birkenhead.
We were not going to arrive there in less than a week.
It would days down through the new ports of the Dee, and the steel works there
Then across the land to the Mersey.
I was thinking about this, and about why I was drawn there
To the church where we used to go.
In truth, I had been told to go, and just desired it."

On the way, we would see the two ships laid down in 1975,
Stationed at Birkenhead docks, for sale to the Egyptian navy at the last;
They had served in the Falklands, as dry stores ships,
23,000 tonnes displacement unloaded.
These two enormous military boats,
Armed with only a few machine guns,
And some anti-rocket gatling guns, were sailing by.

"Where exactly are we going, dad?" my son asked.
"We are on our own again, and wherever you want to go,
it looks like it's a long way."
And I asked him: "Where do you want to go?
We've just been walking, now, and the country
Is getting more real, like it used to be.
I think we should go home" he said.
"What about, if we walk through the country now, not by the sea.
Down to Llangollen where we used to go
And get home that way?
I do not get tired. Do you get tired?" he said turning to his sister.

So we went south, over the hills of Clwyd,
Heading for the vale of Llangollen.
I wanted to approach home, and settle down.
"We'll approach home from the west,
Following the Dee".

As we were walking, a man joined us.

We had not seen any settlements. It might have been any era.
And yet, the land was cultivated and tidy,
And there were hedges and fences and pathways.
"Who are you", I said.
"I am that William Law who, many years ago,
You read about, and wanted to imitate
In spiritual ritual prayer, I had discovered in England.
But the fires lit by one can spread to many.
And this most important technology
Can also be forgotten entirely and snuffed out.
I had advised prayer in secret, in community with God,
Voiceless and Godlike. But my little candle was not seen by the people of
England
And did not set many others alight."
"How can such technology be spread today?
And how can we stop the fire and light from being extinguished?" I asked him.
He said: "Such prayer is always going on now.
It is as if, we are alive
And always the prayer is being said, in front of us, as a community.
Let us say with our whole soul and with our whole mind, let us say.
Lord, have mercy.
And yet," he went on, "a church of the body of Christ is still needed,
To fill the cathedrals,
And became an order and hierarchy are wanted
In order to carry on the search for higher levels of good; it is possible
And is rewarded."

He explained to me that the church has also been recreated,
Just as it was, in heaven.
It was created, the role of patriarch, metropolitan, bishop, priest and deacon.
And the places where they would work and do service.
Not as something separate from the normal
But as an enjoyment, like dancing.

"My companion is the Englishman, Michael Faraday
The great instinctive experimenter.
Our common opponent then was not ignorance
But the devil.
That is all over, since Christ trampled down death, and overcame the devil.

This road, we take, would have been called a waste or desert in my day".

81

Now the land was rolling hills, with some wheat fields
And the kind of desert places where the English poet Spencer
Once set his Red Cross knight.
Green everywhere, broken by some old stone walls,
Violent flowering ferns covering some hillsides,
And copses and the promise of a forest.
That is how it all was, and don't forget the little streams
Cutting down the hills every few hundred meters.
A road now and again; maybe an old railway line
Light rain, and a bit misty in the lower and higher regions
But nothing is too high up.
It is God's country.
Our group went south, with Law and Faraday as well,
Heading for the Cistercian Abbey
At Llangollen and the hill top castle there,
Built by the same Christians who founded the abbey.
And in England, from these waste and rural places,
There have come people of great power, to join with others in the cities,
Like Dr Johnson, who I met a long time ago, as the world ended.
And also Shakespeare. "O Dad, I would really like to meet Shakespeare" said
my daughter.
"Who brought together all the old stories and scraps of plays,
And made them work
With his magical power of words!"

"I don't know if I like the idea of just calling for people" I said.
The sun was very high and bright in the sky.
We went through an ancient oak forest. Mr Law said:
"In the days before the end of everything,
There was a need for educating men in chivalry and virtue,
Men who were in no hurry to become monks.
And these things are instilled in men's hearts today, at their creation,
Because they please God. There is no need for national armies in this age
But, there is still the virtue of the violent man who has learned to be gentle,
Because this nature is in a man. I am sure,
That Shakespeare, who was obsessed by the nature of man in nature,
And as civilised creation, will walk with us."

Although, we prayed God, there was no materialisation of the bard.

There were others marking way and singing:
"O Lord our God, accept this fervent supplication from Thy servants,
and have mercy upon us according to the multitude of thy mercies;
and send down Thy compassions upon us and upon all Thy people,
that await of Thee abundant mercy."

"Where are they all going? Did all people just get revived?" I said
"Are they all travelling home, like me?" I asked the children. "You know more
than me."

"There is no saying that Shakespeare survived,
or that he is able to move around in time and space, like the saints," I said.
"We should pray for him. Know he kept God in secret
In his dangerous time.
This paradise or heaven is the same as the old world,
Except with less distance from God; and so that we are protected from
temptation.
And, finally, where people are healed and do not die.
As if Christ were everywhere, and had healed all of us.
I wish that Christ would assist and bring him" I said.

"I will not impose on anyone else, afterwards, again."
And that evening, we ate some of the fruit growing around the place, drank,
Smoked a pipe,
And through the forest, the dramatist came wandering to find us.
Also, came Maxwell, the physicist, who worked with Faraday's experiments
And framed them in mathematical laws.
Those two talked warmly; and also Shakespeare and I,
With my family listening.

82

I led us south, and William Law came, with Faraday, and also Shakespeare.
Mr Maxwell was not so fond of the forest and went his own way.
It occurred to me, that perhaps we were not all engaged on the same route,
And that the minds and even the reality of some of the voyagers were not the same as mine.
For why would they spend time coming to the hills of Clwyd.
"Reality is generally what it appears to be, although opinions differ
And minds can be damaged" said Shakespeare.
I am here, with you, because we have as much time as we could possibly want.
You are in a hurry, to get home. And once there, you might understand.
But, I have taken your path already, too,
And know that there are heights and depths waiting."

We went across various crossings of streams, and around hills and brakes,
Then came finally to a hilltop from which I could see a large body of water
Which was obviously Bala or Llyn Tegid, the source of the Dee.
So we went there, and determined to follow the Dee to Chester.

We prayed for the dead, when we got there;
The ones who did not make it.
And that they be forgiven for their transgressions.

I began to think of my wife, who I knew to be alive,
And had agreed to meet us,
And I wished that she was with her son.
We sat down at the side of the lake,
where there used to be a boat house and training centre
Where I had gone as a cadet student of the army as a child.

There was a house still there, and we went inside for the night.
I imagined my wife, with her son. Perhaps they were in Bulgaria.
Or in Portsmouth, where her son had wanted to visit to see HMS Victory
Nelson's ship.
I explained to my children: "I am sorry we are taking this long route,
And rushing to get home. I can't wait to see
The last stages of this revelation, and to begin living.
A man needs a home; and I need to know there is something.

And I can't understand my good fortune.
How my faith that this impossible thing would be has been rewarded!
When Nelson, whose victories were miraculous
Against the French and other Navies of Napoleon,
Died having been shot, he said many times: 'Thank God I have done my duty'.
Nothing hurts a human more, than to have failed to keep his word,
Or failed to have done his job. His reputation is what he is.
That is the immortal part of him in people's minds.
Separate from his profession or actions, is the integrity and control over himself
So he does what he says he will and should.
See, a man lives a conceptual life, needing meaning."
"Yes, dad, this is why, even though there is no need
For health and doctors in this era now,
God has provided us with the profession of medics."
"Where and how do you know?" I said.
They laughed.

83

"I will grow up. I was told by Jesus, when I woke up" she said.
"And I will go to school, with other children.
Children will be born, and grow up. And then they might go to university.
The great schools of Oxford and Cambridge are open to us,
Or are being filled with their doctors.
And medicine, taught at the University of Liverpool, is one of the courses.
We don't know everything. So people will have to study.
Here in eternity they will have to learn. There is a great deal to learn, endless."
"Do you think, they will have to study things like theology?
Or do people already know God?"
"They will study theology," my son said. "I want to do that."

We were not alone, even though it seemed that way.
From the heavens or some place, we could hear
"Pray, ye Catechumens, to the Lord".
And the joyful response:
"Lord, have mercy".
We slept, and in the morning, we set off. We said goodbye to the
electromagnetic genius,
He shook hands warmly, reminding us that keen learners built the modern
world
And that God loved them for it.

Also, William Law decided to stay around Bala, while we set off, in a boat
Toward Chester. Shakespeare came with us, silent and watchful of the places.
Within a couple of hours we arrived at the rocks outside the town
Overlooked by Dinas Bran.
The frothy waters were not in spate.
We disembarked at the town, which was populated, and walked to the Abbey
Which had been rebuilt after five hundred years as a ruin.

We could hear a service going on inside.
High on the hill, there was the castle, and the school where I once taught.

84

In the town, they had started at industry, producing things.
Though the Welsh usually mined things, copper, slate, lime, lead, coal
They were making boats, small things for the water, from timber,
And clothing, many old industries.

We left Shakespeare to look around by himself.
I shook his hand and he embraced all three of us.

I explained about the old small boats and canoes they used to make here
And use on the river;
"The plastic, which was considered a painful blight on the world,
Used to come from the oil refineries in the Wirral;
The oil was extracted by suction from the North sea,
And was piped there to be refined.
They used fractional distillation, to get various parts of the oil separated out.
In a cooling tower, they would heat the oil,
And watch as the lighter parts floated to the top.
Those parts or liquids would be siphoned off.
Some elements of the carbon oil, to be found underground,
The squashed and petrified remnants of old life,
Could be modified with other elements
So that they could be dried, and they became very durable
Substances. Heated again, manufacturers could melt them,
And cool the plastic into shapes
The shape of bottles or the like.

But the use of carbon, and all the other things which came,
Thousands of things, from the distillation, of oil,
And the separation out of the constituents,
Is no longer needed, I think".
We sat at a shop, and drank tea together.

"O Lord our God, who dwellest on high
And lookest down on things that are lowly,
Who unto the human race hast sent forth salvation,
Thine Only-Begotten Son and God our Lord Jesus Christ:
Look upon Thy servants the catechumens."

"Dad, we are alive again, and we have nearly reached home.
Now, we are still learning, and the second stage of the education will start.
Shall we stay here for a day, before getting home?
We can see the river side, and the park, like we used to."
My daughter said this. I prepared my mind for what was to come.

After our dinner, the three of us walked to the forest at the top of the hill
Where the castle was. It was still derelict at the time.
In the woods on the hill
We met a man, who lived alone in there, it seemed.
"I had lived until now, sometimes afraid of the seriousness of life,
Loving the forest, and living out there, like an outlaw perhaps.
There will be no need for the legend of the free rebel Englishman, now,
When the crown belongs to a good man who knows how to govern,
A monarch, a real man to govern men with justice and common sense.
And the church is not run for anything else but God's worship
And the benefit of all. It will be merry England again."

I cannot say who this man had been
Because I failed to give him reply or to ask.
For all I know, it was Robin Hood, or Blaise Pascal
So enamoured of true spiritual solitude.

85

After examining the valley below the castle from that viewpoint,
I knew for certain that the Earth had been created just as it had been

We resumed the journey by boat, back in the valley
And so we came to England, as the Dee brought us over the border.

"In the physical world, which is bound by law
Any organisation of electrons forming a charged force which can be used
Needs to obey two rules:
First, that work is needed to make a force useful and organised,
And work means turning disorganised energy into directed energy, which
releases heat
And, second, the electrons and electrical charge will become disorganised and
useless inevitably, when work is completed
The ordered energy is not maintained, but eventually becomes useless and tends
toward cold.
Work goes in to forming the useful energy
And work is done by the useful stored energy made in this way
To become useless and dissipated.

The history of mankind, is the story of how
Pyramids of power and people were made
Dressed up in uniforms and hieratic symbols
With the single intent, of ordering people, to do work
And offer their energies in a directed way.

Work to ensure that food would grow, and that animals could be raised and be
slaughtered,
Work to build monuments and shelters,
Work to steal land and destroy enemies,
Work to maintain a decent orderliness in a household.

Men discovered, that coal and oil, and wood, and gas
Represent ordered force, capable of being burned and creating the heat energy
Very easily.
So, the fuels replaced the labouring muscles of men."

So spoke my son, to me.

"And that is why slaves were no longer useful in later times.
And, because energy is not restricted by God and nature today
There are no slaves, nor any need to form the grand hierarchies of nation state
order
To produce and harness the people's energies."

"What?", I said, "will there be no more need to dig, and burn for fuel
Or any need to pay for it, the fuel and the saving of us
From slavery and enchainment to other men?"

"That is right, dad", he said.

Then I started talking about things which interest me,
The mechanical fuel driven engine, as follows:
"The pistons and engines made of metal, they work without need for fuel,
And they do not run out by the laws of thermodynamics,
Or heat loss and energy dissipation.
Do they remember what a piston is, and how,
Even their most extravagant works of transportation,
Making a journey of weeks take barely a few hours?
Do they make all the parts here, from steel,
Which is iron with some carbon mixed in?
A piston will turn a wheel, by responding to a fire's heat.
It consists of a tube, at the bottom of which is a source of heat,
And a cylinder which moves up and down inside it.
On top of the moving cylinder there should be an arm
Attached to a cam wheel, a pear shaped wheel.
A fire under the cylinder, will move it upwards, still inside the tube,
And the arm will go up, moving the arm, which moves the cam wheel,
And finally the cam will turn the main wheel
Of a vehicle, or anything else you want to do some work.
As the cylinder moves up, it lets out a bit of the force which sent it upwards,
So that it can go down again, so that it can repeat the cycle from the start.
And so on, until the machine breaks, or the fuel runs out for the fire.
Use two or three cylinders, for more power and fluent motion
To drive that main wheel."

I remember, that even my daughter told me, about the nature of life for a man:
"The aim of a man's life, before, was to keep himself warm, or cool
And free from hunger;
And to get a place in the social hierarchy which gave him respect and employment.
But now, we can say
'We thank Thee, O Lord God of Hosts,
Who hast vouchsafed us to stand even now before Thy Holy Altar'
And we are fed, warm, valued, and know the meaning of ourselves."

Later, having passed through Bangor, and past the site of the lost castle at Holt,
We got off the boat at the estate of the Duke of Westminster,
And walked through the forest along the Dee.
That Duke, who owned the lands around central London,
As well as these, his ancestral homelands.
But note, he had no relation to the feudal Norman owners of the land
Who took it by force at the conquest.
We found the duke at the river bank, fishing.

And I think, that it was nearing the time, when I would see more clearly;
And there were forces and powers of God, not energies of nature,
At work to stir my soul to action, for I heard, as it were from behind the screen of reality
From deep inside the nature of physical things:
"We thank Thee, O Lord God of Hosts,
Who hast vouchsafed us to stand
Even now before Thy Holy Altar"

86

I was confused to see the old Lord of this place,
A member of the Lords before resigning or giving it up
In the Blair destruction of our constitution
When the Blair government also split up Wales and Scotland from Britain.
Although, it is known universally that aristocratic rulers
With their honesty, barbarity, and paternalism
Tend to make better politicians,

He had a net for the fish, and sat by the river. I was surprised saying:
"I thought you were dead; I did not expect to see you again"
And he said: "We are all dead now
And reborn or recreated."

"Do you still live here, in your hall? What about your ancestors, do they also
dwell here?"
"They do" he said.

"You wrote to me, once, asking for employment in my household
As a poet and artist, as if you were Goethe looking for
A relationship of patron and poet and artist.
Nothing like that was going on at the end of the world.
Your hopes, like mine in those days, were always to lead you to nothing."

"We joined the Army at the same time, and left together, you at the top
Me at the bottom."

"I enjoyed it for the friends, the way a man there
Was what he was made from, in his mind and his bodily strength.
A duke was generally no better than the next man,
It was clear and obvious, to me, a part time soldier, it was good for me."

I sat down with him, and the children played on the bank of the river
Going after butterflies, and picking flowers.

"And there is time for poets today, too
Don't think, that the world has no more aspiration to learn,
And expand the mind. Poetry is the expansion of the mind in a musical form of

language.
It is for school children who are forced to learn,
And for people who want to learn;
It is that kind of consciousness and intelligence
Which can't express itself and doesn't want to express itself.
It is secret and almost undying
So the person who is a poet is cursed to say the unsayable.
To be set aside.
I told you I did not want your poetry or friendship or to employ you back then
How could a poet be employed, anyway?
I am sorry that that particular prohibition of our age
That poets can't be paid or employed,
Was too strong for me, and I turned you away."
I said nothing about that.
"We have been at the source of the Dee, and saw hardly anyone
But what will we find in the town?
Are all the dead alive there?" I asked him.

"Of course there are people, but not all.
There has been a gigantic sacrifice, and all them that arose from their tombs
And reassembled in their flesh and bone selves,
Most of them fell back into nothing.
But at the city gates, you'll find them.
Revived, educated for heaven."

We left the Duke, and walked along, past the scene of the battle of Chester
Which happened some fifteen hundred years ago,
When the Saxon invaders
Met the old Christian Welsh at the Dee, of the old Celtic faith
Before the coming of the new Christianity from Rome and Byzantium.
And famously, the monks from Bangor were cut down, every one
While the fight was going on, though they were in prayer.

At last, we came to the city walls, and the grand houses,
Lining the river. We could see our old house on the Mount,
Where Charles I's defending soldiers withstood the Parliamentary advance for a
few hours.
In those cruel times, when the non-aristocratic parliamentarians,
Pushed aside the land-owning and Tory barons of the old England.

Outside the house, the burning place,
Where Protestant and Catholic had both their places of martyrdom,
Remembered with a granite needle. Our house was just there,
By the church of St Paul, with its decoration by William Morris.

But, the good and the bad are redeemed in heaven,
And Parliament and Crown and the true Church are not confused.

We came up Foregate Street.
At the city gates, at the boundaries, my children and I could see the city was busy
And at the gate, an alarm was sounded for us.
Out from the guardhouse came a man dressed in white with a red cross woven in it.

An old king loyal to God and his country, Henry Vth, they called him.
He ordered:
"Before entry, bend the knee, and lower your head.
It is true, but God has saved us, and there is happiness in communing with him."
And we did as he asked
"Again and often times we fall down before Thee,
O Good One and Lover of mankind."

87

"That king took back his lands from the French
And is described in Shakespeare;
With his Welsh archers and their bows from Welsh ash trees.
It used to be the case, that
Land and property were clearly essential for us to live in and on and for.
But a king could honour God or not, to suit himself.
Now, it is the opposite case. God is essential for us to live in and on and for,
While the use of the town and the land is freely elected for."

Henry was perhaps the first King who recognised this place as his home.
Other kings had thought of it as a source of revenue,
A possession. For him England and Wales was a homeland.

He bowed to me and the children, and we each kissed his hand.
At the city walls, there were men with banners, of the sun
And of the cross, three of them, strong and happy to defend God
with these objects like those which they used
to waft air on a king in hot places. Like big feathers.
They were like the cherubim guarding God's throne in heaven
Assembled around the king, as God is described in Isaiah.
This is the defence of the place they made:
"None is worthy among them that are bound with carnal lusts and pleasures,
to approach or to draw nigh, or to minister unto Thee,
O King of glory, for to serve Thee is a great and fearful thing
even unto the heavenly hosts themselves."

I came into the city at the gate where the old amphitheatre was,
And where the parliamentarians had blown a hole in the walls
With cannon in the old times,
Where there's a new gate to the south west.
But now the Crown and Parliament are one in divine reason.

"The place is old buildings and walls, and remains
But God has made it so. Engineering and building
And care of the stone and the red sandstone structures. "

"How can old titles and hierarchies still endure when there is no need for

them?"
I asked. "Nobody explained to us that there is no need for them," my son said.
"How can a man's heart be aimed at God, and his mind be God's mind
In an act of prayer, if he does not know how to live in time and space for a while
And in time and space, nobody is happy unless there is rank, and aspiration
Humility and service.
We know that the lowest man has as much or more love from God.
The kings, if anything, have here, the duty which makes them unhappy.
They rule, and know that any pride about it is devastating for them.
For the First are now Last, the Last are First.
The two kings of Sparta, the kings or Rome and Athens, and Macedonia,
And if Christian Europe show that a single ruler is the natural way.
Even if there is no direct rule, a human being
At the head of things was always best; instead, frequently
As time went on, they put an empty paperwork bureaucracy at the head.
A devastating loss for any nation."

When I was inside the city, I remembered waiting at the Eastgate
And making my way to the Magistrates court, and the Family Court,
And the other places of a spiritless rule by officials,
Places of undetermined and unending conflict,
Lacking pity and compassion or understanding,
Places of great illogicality in the old days.
Where state employees with no faith or right in them
Had harassed me and my children
Like a fake monarch, lacking any personality or sense
So that not even the Member of Parliament, Chris Matheson,
Could find any way out for us.
Threatening our home and livelihood and physical freedom.
All those problems were gone, and I held my clever children tightly, rejoicing.

On the day of the end of the world, I had been debating exile
To escape the arrests I had suffered for false claims against me.
And the thefts of my money from my bank by the state.
And the threats against me that I would be evicted from my house by local
solicitors
Who were acting with their indifference to morality
On account of my mistakes in contracts of marriage.
Not to mention, the continuous fear of seeing my children back then,

In case the Police had threatened me and them
Lest the state's workers had complained against me.
They were paying my former wife, because she was mad.
And they did her work for her,
Knowing in this way, that she was exactly mad.
I had resolved to fly from the country
But in no part of the world
Was there an organised state which honoured God
And I was going to be alone and ruined,
I was looking, in those days, for a way out of it all
Out of the country or out of life.

88

We walked the short distance, then to the Cathedral
Once hardly more than a tourist attraction
Its dark corners and precincts had comforted me.
Founded by the Norman bishops, and where St Anselm had served
Later Archbishop of Canterbury under the first William.

The man at the door was dressed in white robes, and met me and my children
"I am St Augustine of Canterbury.
Founder of the Church, archbishop, welcome home.
And, you know, that when we look at God, if we can bare to do so
For it is the same as looking at the sun,
You know, that there, are all things, at once,
Unfolding, hiding, exploding into life.
And his created world is the same but in a gentler form.
All things are there, but hidden and revealed piece by piece to a man's sight.
God has simply arranged it, that it should be for the benefit of both
By his love for us.
The creator has remade us to be explorers and for exploration.
And first, we are explorers of our origins and our home.
You, me, and this town, and city". That was how he spoke.

My son added:
"We are to be explorers; but not so much bound
By the age of gravity and electromagnetism,
And those times where energy had to be won by pain and sweat
And to be dissipated and lost."

We walked now, to the altar, and the nave of the Cathedral
With the iconostasis in front.
The priest, in the shady grove which is our cathedral,
Was the ancient King, and human precursor to the Son of God,
Who I would not get to speak to, nor presume.
That King David of the psalms, the first king, and priest.
He was praying for the land and the hierarchy.

"The much suffering English Land and its Orthodox people
Both in the homeland and in the diaspora;

This land, its authorities and the faithful that dwell therein,
May the Lord God remember in His Kingdom,
Always, now and ever, and unto the ages of ages.
All those who are sick and suffering.
Those whose lives are filled with anxiety."
Thus the old king and prophet.

When we retreated from that great stone forest clearing,
With its shadowy places for meeting with the most high,
And the quiet echoing inadvertent holiness
Gorgeous in itself, the seclusion of its darkness
Like the inadvertent beauty of the noise of an orchestra,
Whether playing in harmony or tuning up and simply making a noise,
I remarked:

"The light from the candles and the glass.
You make glass from sand, silica ground up sand,
It must be heated with a hot kiln fire to nearly 2000 degrees,
Adding the ashes of plants, known as potash,
Will lower the temperature needed.
But if you do that, you must also add the dust of limestone,
To stop the glass from leaking.
Don't you? Where do we find lime in Britain? What does it look like?"

My son replied:
"Lime is used in mortar for bricks; it is an alkali;
Get limestone white stones, and heat and burn them
Until they fall apart, and become quick lime.
As a fire rages around the dust in a kiln,
Take the dust, and add some to the glass you are making.
It will be molten when hot; so it can be poured into a shaped mould,
Or played with and blown into shape with the lips."

On the ceilings of the church were the great banners and colours
Of the greatest of the line infantry, Royal Welch Fusiliers,
Who served across the globe. The founder of that regiment was there,
Of Cherbury, Lord Herbert, stood at ease,
Beside the passionate defender of British freedom and integrity,
Maggie Thatcher, the Prime Minister.

My daughter, years absent from me, was there,
She who was small, and delicate, and clever, and good.
Who had been cruelly taken from me in the old life,
Denying her my help to learn and grow up
In many of her first years. But all of that was over
That unceasing subterranean unease.
We were ready for a new life.

89

"That the whole day may be perfect, holy, peaceful, and sinless,
We have asked for this day, and every day to be the same in that regard"
My son said. "And we say 'Lord have mercy'.
We'll go now, walk back home, dad".
We walked out of that mighty red building, and into the town.
"It's the promise of the future, which you loved about us, your children.
I know that very well. You were always coaching and looking at us in your imagination,
Seeing there what we might become,
You wanted us to be stronger and better than you."
I replied: "And that cannot fail to be the case now".

We went home, which was outside the walls.
The city was warm, and sunny
And the day was perfect and peaceful.
"You know, the fault in the way things were,
When you couldn't see us
And nothing worked in Britain
Was that the state and government always fails.
Like, the failure of the labour and industry of Britain
When the state was in charge of them.
The factories were taken over by the unions and then government,
And the industry of mining, and energy, failed when the crown tried to run them
With the officials and the servants of the crown.
And the trains, were torn up from the ground, irreplaceable, by those same people.
The education of children became political and became mere child minding
When the crown's state officials were in charge of it.
Finally, the army was run down into nothing
But ceremonial work for politicians;
And why does it surprise you, if the police failed
And the courts, supplied by the same people?"

"What is the alternative?"
"The individual man, of course, in the form of a monarch,
Or in the form of an individual free man

Who agrees to work with others, or not, at his discretion.
And he loves himself and his country
So he has motive to do only good, or do nothing.
The state has got no motive, it is no one."

There were bumble bees in the flowers at the side of the road,
And they sought out their nests in the ground;
While their fertilisation of the flowers and crops went on
Without poisons or pesticides.
The little mammals, the hedgehogs and the birds were under no threat
In our gardens and hedges.

There were no historic animals from the stone age,
They had not been revived.
There was a parade of the second most important saint
And the second greatest infantry regiment of Britain
St David of Wales, and the Parachute Regiment, with their red berets
Going along with the drums, out of the city, ahead of us.

90

"There will be saints, and the requirement for men and women
who are more devoted to God than others.
That is how it is. And they will remain hidden out of the way,
As they did, but yet more so. In this heaven
There is need of men and women to devote themselves to God
In constant prayer, trying every moment to be closer to him
And like him." This is what my son said.

"And is that what you want to do in time, son?" I asked him.

"We should say, of ourselves that
We are a sacrifice, and we ask God that our sacrifice
May be acceptable, and that the good Spirit
Of His grace may rest upon us, and upon these Gifts set forth,
And upon all His people.
How could it be otherwise, Dad? What is the highest? I want to find that;
I want to know the truth, and the creator of the world is a person as an infinite thing
To be explored. Who would deny himself this, as his mission?
And, if you can be like the Son of God, and not be misled or die failing to do it,
Then, I see clearly, and feel love for this idea."

And now, the Saint of Wales, caught up with us as we walked and talked together,
He came running up after us as we left the town
Seeing that we were newly arrived.
He began talking with my daughter
Who wanted to know medicine and science:

"In the substance of all things are atoms, tightly bound, irreducible.
No chemical process can undo an atom which nature and God has bound together
In the inside of a star. A Gold atom is chemically immortal,
and was born inside stars and massive heavenly bodies.
Molecules are formed chemically from such atoms, and can be undone again.
So if you mix gold with something else, to thin it out, and make the gold go further,

It can be extracted out again, pure.
I was the water drinker, the leek eater,
No drunkard and a vegetarian,
I gave the soldiers of Wales my blessing, and their symbol."

We came to our home, near the water works,
Where the Romans had wells from ground water stores,
And the Victorians had built the water tower
An ancient area of springs,
And the canal runs nearby, the Dee down below on the plain, down 50 meters
The front door. Our saint also came in with us.

"The atoms whether gold, or tin, or zinc, or salt, or whatever,
Do form they bind to each other to make new compounds,
As water is oxygen atoms with hydrogen atoms.
The new molecule makes a thing, water,
Which is nothing like what it was made of,
Namely, two gases.

They are helped in this joining, by changes in temperature.
They bind with their electric charges.
They expand in heat, and make room for each other.
And they change their form in changes of temperature,
So the gas of water becomes liquid
And if you cool it more, it becomes a solid.
Chaotic as gas, randomly moving, expanding and taking up more room."

We came to the front door of our house, the dear protection
Of the domestic life inside, sacred and normal,
Daily life, secret between our small tribe
Both closed and open in the doors.

91

Inside, we found Galya, as if by the pulling aside of the curtain of reality,
To reveal the simplest and purest of love's sources.
And I said to my son,
"The domestic love of a wife, loyal, principled
Soft and yielding. She is an industrious woman, and kind
She looks attentively for the good and pleasant things in our life,
She encourages them, with her candles and icons in the house
As well as the kitchen, and the rooms of various uses.
So, we have to show, with reason and care, an orderly devoted love to others.
She is not your mother, but it is enough."
My son kept his own mind about the home with her in charge of it.

Galya had been waiting, and had made dinner for us.
St David ate with us, and blessed the house,
Just as the priest of our Christian church had done so many times in the old days.
He spoke as follows, while we sat around:

"From the belief in the Father, creator, by whom all things were made
And from the Son, begotten not made, of one essence with the Father,
Who came down from heaven, and was crucified for us,
And who rose again
And from the Holy Spirit, who spoke by the prophets
We have our church, and by the church have been taught and been worthy
Of being raised from the dead.
Now, the search and the devotion can go on.
In the company of the revived saints,
and in the power of our promise of being God's friends and sons.
As ferocious in this as Fidel Castro, whose atheism defied the United States
But as faithful and in league with the maker, as St John Baptist, the forerunner.

These aren't exactly people who had a family. They were isolated, the saints.
And put aside the procreative life, with a shared bed, children.
But thank God that we have been allowed to enter heaven
with family and merely human loves
As well as the higher austere devotion."

92

The saint went on: "And childbirth is also blessed
Despite the curses laid on it by the Indian mystics who said
That life is a curse, and the Catholics
Who forbade their priests any marriage
Who called physical love a sin and a failure of the spirit
A failure to remain indifferent to the body.
They should never have pried in such holy matters;
How can there be a Son of God, unless there is childbirth?"

My wife had made food of five types, as they eat at Christmas, in the Orthodox
East,
And we were planning to leave a bit for the dead overnight
Though there were no longer any dead. All were revived.

The demons which afflict women in their rages and emotions
They are known.
And what about the damage caused to minds by abusive parents?
These were suffered by the parents of some children
And the demonic curse of hatred for people
Was passed from generation to generation, mother to children.
But those devils are gone.
The enjoyment of tormenting each other, between man and woman, woman and
man
Is a thing of the past.
They are forgiven, and evaporated, like gas from a liquid
When the liquid is heated.
While those demons are condensed again in the lake of fire.

My boy said: "Here Saint David, is where dad used to pray
The icon corner. Tell us, how to pray",

And the saint said:
"When you pray, close the eyes, and be still and immovable,
And call on the name of Christ, in silence
And simply breath in and out, saying Jesus's name,
Only until there is complete peace in the mind
And you are refined and above your life, your mind, your personality.

So we attune easily to God.
Stay so, and you will see: how the higher reaches of heaven open to us.
So, see, here St John the Evangelist
Amongst us, in the great city not of this town
But God's own company."
We could hear some singing a triumphal hymn, shouting:
"Holy, Holy, Holy;
Heaven and earth are full of thy glory;
Blessed is he that cometh
In the name of the Lord. Hosanna in the highest."
When it was late, and dark outside, we slept.

93

Having called to remembrance all the Saints,
Remember that we are just flesh and blood, which God has made
And which he did so, through a woman and her body.
But the body is not what they used to call physical.
There is use for knowing how objects are made
And what they are.
And, if anyone wonders, among my readers
If there is something smaller than the almost invisible atoms
Then, there is, because the atom has a nucleus of particles with a mass
And a certain atomic number is the number of those particles
And every atom for instance, nickel or helium, is different from any other
By the number of mass particles it has. That makes it weigh more or less than
other substances
And makes all the difference for its other properties.
But can we turn an atom of 16 particles into one with 8?
Yes, but a nuclear force is holding them together very strongly.
But now, that you know the secrets of all mankind, let us see the easiest miracle
Where the human being and mankind come from
Which is the mother and her motherhood.
And the mother is not just a body, or an object.

"An awesome power given to men and women in particular
Which should be sheltered and respected
But which the lustful and the degenerate last days of men celebrated
With sexual adventures, the equivalent of black magic and destroying nature
Curtailed by abortions and murder of infants.
They mistreated their womenfolk, telling them to behave like men,
And destroying their womanliness.
Let men be men, and leave women to their own roles.

Any man who has not been a soldier is no real man
He has been hanging around the house and peace too long
Becoming a woman, and making his wife into a man."
My son said this, and the Saint blessed him for it.

Now it was time to prepare to meet God.
I left my children and left my wife, at home

It was time to make first steps to meet the infinite, and to face God.

St David led me out, and put on the medals I had won in life for the Queen
He led me out into the street; I made my way to Wrexham
And the barracks of the military. I was alone now.
I was saying goodbye to all of this.
Across the fields of the villages along the way, in Rossett and Gresford, I went
And came to the mill and the Victorian barracks. I walked all that way.

There, various officers and soldiers were meeting one another,
And a friend, and writer of the Welch was there,
Along with Robert Graves and Siegfried Sassoon, and David Jones
All Royal Welch like us; my friend was Geraint Jones:
"There is no shame and no virtue in the military of the old way now
But the virtues of the soldier remain essential".

94

The University of Oxford and the one at Cambridge,
Have not been able to show that Fatherhood is anything
Except a natural law for all things which must be born.
The Father shows the way, and cares for his children."

I saw in the barracks, the battle honours of my battalion,
And the campaigns I had been involved in
For my country, my island, in Europe and Asia.
Old members of my battalion were also there, drawn by the same demand,
Having been born again, and wanting to ensure
They knew that the old life had survived in some ways.
Some griefs and shame and guilt meant, that we did not talk too much.

"I must," I said to my old friend from the war in Iraq, Geraint,
"Go to the church, in Birkenhead
And see whether I can find the priest, and diligently find out how he is"
"Your chapel was too far away from where you had your home,
Because Orthodox churches were hard to find.
So, walking will be a long way," he said.

"I know that. But I will walk for all that.
As we used to on our long patrols in the Brecons. I'll go
Where the priest does the work year after year
Fulfilling the calendar, and keeping the doors open
In national emergencies, during orders to shut, whether persecuted, or
honoured
He has done God's work without fail, in open celebration, in secret,
And kept the lights on
For the saints om the old world.
But is it still the case now?"

I began walking, from Wrexham, back to Chester, and then up the Wirral
Where the poet of Sir Gawain and Green Knight,
Is known to have lived and composed,

I was joined along the way, by another, going to the church
To meet one of the last living priests of the faith;

Himself long dead.
He was stood at the side of my path, and waited for me
And then held out his hand and said:
"You are Nicholas, baptised Jason, and chrismated as Nicholas,
I am the brother of the Lord, James."

I was concerned to be alone, and was embarrassed.
"I was with your brother, Jesus, for some time, at the end of the world," I said.
But that seemed natural, because I was dying.
Now, it is as if life is normal again, and important men like you
Should not waste your time with me.
Please, sir, don't waste your time on me", I begged him.

But he explained that he was here for the creator
And not for me. "It is necessary, that people are watched and taught
In their first moments in heaven," he said.
I accepted this, and we talked.
He told me, in answer to my question,
That he was there at that moment
When they asked Jesus, when he was on Earth in the old days,
How to pray: "And Jesus had said:
Our Father, who art in the heavens.'"

"Sir" I asked him, "Did they sometimes get it wrong in their story of Christ
Missing things out, or telling things not as they were?
Those who later wrote the Gospels?"

"Of course" he said. "They wrote years after it all.
And they missed out most of his life.
And of course, they failed to understand
Or explain exactly the meaning of it.
But that is natural. But what they did tell about, that did happen,
The healings, the preaching, the last meal, and that he died and we saw him
Not many days later, desolate as we were before.
All this is true."
"But the gospels are not the word of God but of men."
"How else do we allow translations?
Or, why were many gospels fraudulent, and discarded?
And why were there malicious gospels, or heretical?

The four which survive can be trusted, as human recollections of a hard subject."

We walked on, heading north.

95

When night fell I was still walking, with the brother of the Lord.
For the first time, I saw the lights of the stars, and the planets.
They had not been in the sky when I was first released from the state of judgement.
"You are looking at the sky, wondering if the stars have just been created.
And the answer is, yes, they are recently created again.
Every aspect of the world is built at his Will.
They have no immediate effect on our solar system,
In the emptiness of all infinite space and yet,
They are there, waiting.
If he did not want or need those heavenly bodies, they would not be there.
And, notice, that while Dante, your poetic guide,
Was wrong about the composition of the heavens,
He was not wrong, that they do contain mysteries and divine intention.
Understand that there is room for exploration
and development in the stars and on other worlds than this."

And now, we came to the estuarial water,
And went up the hill to the village where the church was.
We crossed ourselves and went inside. Where, my spiritual Father was,
Named after the Apostle Paul.
We entered as he was saying the prayer:
"Broken and distributed is the Lamb of God,
Broken, yet not divided; ever eaten,
Though never consumed,
But sanctifying them that partake thereof"
And he was elevating the offering.
I wept to see him still there, doing his work
Through all the years keeping the world at work,
While the world turned around the sun,
By virtue of his selfless honest prayers to God the Father
To keep us inside the horizon of his charity;
Offering to keep the word of God alive among men,
So that, when the end came as it did,
There were enough of us for God to save, because we still knew him.
I stayed at the side, observing the ceremony.
With Father Paul there was the Son himself, at the altar,

Who broke the bread and blessed the wine,
which were then mixed as is the tradition.

There were other familiar people too, who I knew, and they lined up
To be given communion.
Later, they finished the liturgy, and when he had changed into his black simple
robe,
My priest said to me: "We were right all along
Through the darkness of our time,
To form our community and to believe, and to tell ourselves that we knew the
truth.
The doubts in the heart, speaking, were sometimes crushing,
But it was so clear to me, at least," he said,
"That the nature of reality was,
That God spoke to anyone wishing to hear
And advised them that he loved them, and was pushing them gently
To reverse the ancestral sin, be friend to Him
To listen to the conscience and intuition of the mind
Longing for the next world above all,
Not the one we knew."
"Thank you for all you did" I said.
"I am going to go see Liverpool and my old university.
The physical world, the tenets of its priests, the people who said
That we are entirely locked in our little brain,
And meet other people similarly locked in
And that this is the ultimately reality
All of us locked inside a randomly evolved brain;
How they were mistaken.

All the matter is merely compressed energy
All reality merely compressed energy. And this the highest truth for them.
It has so little sense to it, and yet, perversity
Made this vision of things triumph almost over the entire world.
And would have been completely triumphant
If it were not for a few, who built against that storm
And the Apocalypse, as you did."
I embraced him, and left.
The brother of the Lord, James, remained behind.
I went out alone toward the Mersey,

And the tunnel which goes under it at Wallasey.

96

As I left, I heard the voices of the unknown and almighty
God's angels, singing, in praise of my friend and teacher.
They sang about him, where once they sang about the gifts of the table:
"Behold, I approach unto Christ, the immortal King and our God.
Impart unto me an unworthy priest the precious Body of our Lord
And God and Saviour Jesus Christ unto remission of sins
And unto life everlasting."
At the university, on the hill overlooking the town,
Where the Catholic cathedral was standing, all glass and steel,
Paddy's wigwam,
I went looking for my friend and teacher,
At the philosophy department, and the School of English.
I found somebody there, who I did not know, and asked:
"Where is everyone, the young, and the teachers?
The place is empty, as it used to be during a holiday".

The person I spoke to explained to me:
"There aren't many here; the students are at home, and the teachers,
Many did not want to make it through. There, in their rooms,
are Professor Stephen Clarke, and Dr Simms.
But there is grief enough, and it is better
To let the new generation learn from them, slowly, a new world."
"Who are you?" I said. "I am Mary, Magdalene
And I understand the shame of past mistakes,
And how a conversion and turning in the personality
Can be painful and shameful."
I did go to see the Doctor and Professor
High up there, in their towers, the light on,
Each overlooking a square of the university,
Where the other rooms were dark, and the students absent,
High above the city and the waterfront.
Professor Clarke said to me: "We shall rebuild,
Just as it should have been at first. We can bring back
The intellectual understanding of God."
And I said: "I understand, that the technological element of life
Is also important to the Father, and creator.
Christ and Christians have never had any issues with science."

"That is so," he said. "But it is still an effort of generations,
To get used to this situation and to understand.
In my painstaking works of biology and theology,
I mulled these things over, and over. In time."
"Professor", I said, "What you were doing is enough,
And I am grateful. And you were right."

97

There was nothing else for it, but to go home.
To my wife and children. But I was not alone.
Because I was thinking of the Son of God, Jesus.
I confined my thinking to the awareness of being aware
So that I could see that divine thing which God gave us
Always and everywhere. Most difficult of all,
I said: "I want to be the son of God,
Which is what is promised, when all sins are removed
from me or remitted, and I am given everlasting life
Eating the holy body and Blood.
What is easier, then imitating a man who we admire
Who was famous, or rich, and beloved?
And about whom we know many interesting facts?
But so much harder, when the man is not a human only
But strange, and unloved, crucified;
Secret and with a mission to heal and
Who caused misunderstanding,
Whom the powerful and important arranged to be judicially murdered?
Now this is hard, and it is not rewarded
With self-satisfaction, or certainty in a dark place.
Because the son of God gives up his certainty and control
And lets God be his will.
But let your will be done, and as much as possible,
I will live as if I am you and your son, God."

Night fell, and I was tired. Holy night descended on me and the world
Because what God also gave us, is a kindly blindness,
So that we have freedom, and a delicate hold over our own power
Even though, the facts are very much otherwise, and we are responsible.
I remembered, as I was falling asleep in the warm night air,
At the side of the newly made pathway toward Chester and Wrexham
How my nana had loved her son, and held a party at her house
To remember him, years after he had died when still barely a man.
She played his records, and listened to them as he did.
Caring for him, and with complete loyalty to his memory.
She and her husband came to me, in the night:
"Nana, I could not have lived without you,

I don't think I replaced your lost son
When you took me in and made me part of your family."
"The world is built on small and consistent kindness,
Which break on the shores of the hard world like waves
Shifting relentless tides. Come and see us, in Wrexham, before long"
She said. "We are there".

98

In the morning, I arose
I was in the mood to give thanks for our release
I felt that I had been accepted into the kingdom
Of the new order, and heaven,
Having partaken of the holy mystery of Christ
And attained to resurrection.
I was anxious to see the children again, and my wife.
At home, I found the living room transformed
And in a hallucinatory state
I observed that the Queen of England was waiting for me.
The children had invited her
A child's bold request; and it had been answered
By the old and careful monarch.
But in addition, for the time,
We were able to find no distinction between this house
And the palace in London where she spends her time.
"How can this be?" I asked, and bowed
In a way which was probably inappropriate.
"Dad, dad, we went around Chester, and she was visiting; and
There weren't many people around;
And we asked her to come here for something to eat for dinner!"
"Sit, and let us talk" the Queen, Elizabeth the Second, said.
"Like some of the others you have met, as the children have told me you did,
I came here so you can write down what I say
In your poem, for all time.
We have come through the end of the world and judgement.
And we remain bound to the land, and loyalties
Which were in place before.
The Holy Spirit has worked through us all,
And through me in my stewardship of the land,
And has sustained our people, with me as head of the Church.
Owner of lands after conquest, head of government and justice,
In a place which had become for hundreds of years
The dwelling of merely atomised individuals
With each individual bumping against the next,
In a society of madness and exploitation.
All that is over. By virtue of the Holy Spirit,

The age of the nation in the guidance and love of God is arrived."
"What about that dissolute neighbour, who took the Empire
And reduced the world to a client status,
Borrowing traditions, and ideas, without the organic spirit of the people,
And the roots in the soil of Europe?" I said.
"Will international politics still spoil our character
And our belief in providence?"
The Queen shook her head.
"Scarcity of resources and international rivalry
And confusion of cultures, will not be problems.
Let us praise God that we have survived
And continue in the political settlement which we have inherited."
I agreed and bowed my head to the Queen of the United Kingdom.

99

So, the house where we were, as in the mind of God,
Was also the Lower House of Parliament, a church choir.
It was possible to look up and see the history of that place,
And all history and
Perhaps, all future.
Of new worlds, and births, and God pushing and pulling the human race
In a combined motion of God with man, over millions of years,
So that they could understand each other.
"Looking into the light of God, we see everything, dad."
My son, who was eighteen years old, was in full awareness of his reasoning abilities
And could see what I could not:
"You have been travelling around the land by foot
Which is cute, dad; but we are not only physical but spiritual beings.
With power to create and travel, far from Earth, in imagination
And act, with God in mind or not, virtuously, with his power
Because with his will.
We will build a home for ourselves, where God will visit
And be happy".
He was excited. We looked at the great seat
Of human government and church influence
At the lower and upper houses of Westminster,
 "Is it possible," I asked my Queen,
"That we will stray from the path of God's will, so far
As to start the chaos again; but this time, unable to die
And unable to repent of our mistake?"
And she said: "The Mother of God, was obedient to the angel
Who told her, that she would have a child.
There was no questioning, or fear
But she accepted, and submitted.
And bore the maker of the world in her womb.
She is the intercessor for us, to God and to her Son,
On our behalf."
And I was able to see, at the centre of the earth, and in the air
And wherever I turned, so long as I wanted,
The mother of God.
I did not want to turn away,

So I saw how it would be impossible for any one
To rebel against God, seeing the indescribable love
Which he has for any one of us, including me.
"Whoever knows the truth of reality,
And pierces through the fabric, and screen of appearance perhaps
Sees to the inner core of the meaning of things
In the Word, and when he sees, he cannot go wrong.
Everything he does is strong and right
And avoids stupidity and illusion.
The vision of God is the greatest happiness."
From amidst this fumbling guessing at the future, and communal prayer in the spirit
Christ was in our midst, and he joined us in the house, as he did at Emmaus
And said: "We are the inheritance."

100

"Our Father, who delegated to me the power to create the world
I, born and not created,
As a human being in full, and also wholly God,
You created these, who share your mind,
And vision of the Good and the true.
You judged the faulty creation, and cast it out,
Destroyed your enemies,
You gave the freedom to choose the good
To the strong and the weak
Wise and foolish, rich and poor.
In eternity, you have put these people
To be sons of God, like me, and to voyage and explore
To the utmost ends of the possible
And share in your creation;
You made the world beautiful, and strange,
Dangerous and unending,
And based it on compassion
Despite the hardship
And the wilful disobedience of the people;
You gave the means to communicate with you
By simply calling out your name,
And making our petitions to the Theotokos
Daughter of her son;
We here thank you, and ask for vision and knowledge,
And mercy and kindness
The seal of safety against despair,
And the misery of the hopeless.
We, your children, are here."
I looked around me, after looking toward the centre of the cosmos,
And seeing there the meaning of all things
And indeed, all things at once which were created from all time
And from all space.
I saw my daughter and her gentleness,
And my son, a young man of kindness for the weak
With his powerful desire to know God and do right.
They smile and see me. Then I longed to keep our home
And to be together in peace, with my wife

That strong and kind woman who knows how to remember the saints
And keep the house in order. Then, I loved the church
And the Holy Spirit, its founder and its meaning, of which I was part.
And, here was the Queen, the capstone of all order
In the public life out there, and the sure promise
Of decent behaviour among people and nations
A responsible monarch with a human face
Just as God himself seemed in my vision to have a human face;
And having this complete vision I saw
That the mind and heart of God had been given to me.

A note on the verse

The lines are in free verse. The lines are stresses in an irregular rhythm. This tends to bring out the length of syllables, and accentuate the speed of a line. Because the person reading the line is not looking for a specific rhythm, stresses and the length of syllables tends to be more obvious.

Unless there is some kind of rhythm, inside the line, some regularity, the line will simply fall apart, and seem ugly. Perhaps the unexpected rhythm of one line compared with the ones which precede and follow it, is the pleasure to be derived from this form of verse.

In addition, somewhat freed from the easy use of a regular meter, where words can be determined so easily by the exigencies of meeting the number of feet and getting the rhythm, freed from this, the writer of free verse should be able to devote more time to the words themselves. By this, I mean, the words in their accepted usage have a specific set of connotations and a meaning, and the exact word the writer uses, should make use of that. When he is trying to express some idea, he should be looking for the most precise word, and use it in such a way as to make it part of the music and the spell of poetry.

I do not boast that I have followed this principle throughout this long verse work. Maybe long parts of it are not even verse at all, except that they look on the page as if they ought to be. Honestly, this poem could do with work. It is like a draft of ideas, not yet finally crafted. But giving it poetic finish might take a few years, and I am not prepared to wait for publication. If I am given time, I will make amendments in the verse, and the style. The ideas, the philosophy, the story told, are not going to vary in future drafts and years.

Jason Powell

Chester
29.08.2022

Ch	Place	Event	Era	People	Ideas / technology
ARMAGEDDON					
1	Gresford	Nuclear explosions	Today	All dead	Scroll of world is to be rolled up
2	Ruined cityscape	**Christ becomes my leader through this pilgrimage**; corpses risen from the ground	Yesterday	TE Lawrence, St Nicholas of Japan, St Elizabeth the New	Christ says Follow Me
3	Riverside and gate	Movement in space means movement back in time	2,000 years ago	Dr Livingstone	The compass, lenses, basic solar motion
4	Nowhere	The dead rounded up, through a gate		Old Testament prophets, Zizek, Houllebecq, St Symeon the New Theologian	
5		Work parties are formed, to destroy the world. Feeble fall dead again.	5,000 years ago	City of London Corp., Jackie McKay, J.J. Rousseau	
6	Fields sown with salt	World axel tree is pulled down		Bolsheviks, Chomsky, Kissenger	
7	First Horseman, White horse	Megafauna, large animals	6,000 ya	Edward I, Chadwick ancestor, Keel ancestor, Odysseus, Dick Cheyney	
8		Wrecking of megalithic structures and caves	10,000 ya	US Marines, RWF in China	
9		Cave dwellers, first talkers	60,000	Lord Palmerstone, British traders and militia; ancestors on NW frontier	
10		First homo sapiens	120,000	Judge Jeffreys,	
11		Ice ages;	200,000	[Speech about one party state oppression], Donald Trump,	Composition of blood, cells; tempering metals
12	Second Horseman, Civil War				Diseases, basics
13				[Speech, why the dead must see and do these things] NKVD,	Hunger, starvation, basics. Nutrition.
14		Origin of law and consciousness.	250,000	Sulla, Crassus [Speech about Dante's	

		The cave dwellers		vision, compared with this]	
15		Hominids		Achilles, Tax Havens	Organs of bodies, basic anatomy.
16		Depopulating the sea		Thomas a Beckett and church vs. state	Basics of selection and breeding
17	Third Horseman, Black Famine			Cecil Rhodes, Clive of India,	
18		Mammals		Moses,	Money
19				On punishment in the afterlife, Bernard of Clairvaux on Dante	
20				Discourse on Nelson, WWI state of Royal Navy, Bismark	Magnetism and photons; finding position at sea Longitude and Latitude; idea of clock; triangulation
21	Fourth Horseman, Pale, death	All plants, carcasses, and animal remains		Herakles, Griffith ap Ioreth at Criccieth Castle, Mining companies, large tech companies.	Carbon fuels origins; number values; how a day is measured, and Earth around sun
22		Trees and flora	500,000	Welsh princes, uprising of Glyndower	On salt,
23		Insects		Napoleon's army, Goethe, Freud	Carbon and oxygen suffocate the blood; basics of fertilisation; appendix; how to domesticate crops;
24		Water apes		Roy Jenkins, nefarious socialists; DH Lawrence and Frieda;	Water sources, filters, wells
25				NHS, feminism, welfare	
26	The weary chose the lake of fire	Birds	1 million years ago	Wilberforce,	Continental drift
27				Richard Burton explorer; on Ireland and Yeats; Gladstone in Hawarden	
28	Cries of martyrs;				Theory of land ownership
29	Wrexham	Spiders		My sister; grandad;	Theory of kingdom of life; trees,

	Place	Event	Era	People	Ideas / technology
30		Large reptiles	20 mill years ago	Roger Scruton	fungi and moulds, bacteria, anthropods
31		Little mammals		General Percival, Singapore; uncle in that theatre	
32				Slave trade, Captain Cook	How to work out size of Earth; gravity and mass
33		Plague of Darkness		BBC, civil service, Major, Blair, Obama	How they killed the family
34		Trumpets; arrival of great meteor	65 mya	Kierkegaard, Wittgenstein; Adam and Eve	

JUDGMENT

Ch	Place	Event	Era	People	Ideas / technology
1	1st Day	Nativity	70 mya		The atmosphere, its constituents; the temperature scale;
2				Charles Parnell, Plato	Speed of electricity, introduction to electricity; voltage, resistance, amps
3				Derrida, Queen Victoria	
4		[I sleep]		James Joyce (Milton, Tolstoy)	Age of Earth, types of clock
5	2nd Day		100 mya	Duke of Wellington, SA, Redrow	
6				Hill station, Jordan Peterson,	Atomic theory basic, consituents of light as wave or particle; frequency of;
7		Presentation of Christ at the Temple		Nietzsche	Theory of meditation
8		[People who wander out of these oases of festivals die, by choice]		T.S. Eliot	Mass of atoms; gravity related to acceleration;
9				Pericles, Alcibiades, Themistocles; Napier, Lawrence brothers;	Theory of air pressure; layers of earth indicate age;

#	Day	Event	Time	People	Concept
10		Presentation of Theotokos to the Temple		Spencer Beynon;	
11		Exaltation of the Cross	500,000 mya	Rockefellar, Vandebilt, Yeltsin	How to produce steel; lime, iron; brick making; kiln; high temperature fire.
12		Birth of Theotokos	600,000 mya	Raegan; Elwin; soldiers in Europe	
13				Alexander Dugin,	Rainbow, composition of sun: electric plasma or nuclear
14	3rd Day			Ford Motor Co., Wehrmacht. factories	
15		Feast of the Annunciation		De Gaulle, Heidegger	Acids theory;
16 (50)	4th Day	Burial of Theotokos		Geoffrey Hill, RS Thomas. MI6, Peguy	
17	5th Day		800,000 mya	Working class, Simone Weil, St Augustine,	Monarchy as best government
18		The Transfiguration	1 billion years ago	Peter, John, James	
19				Churchill, Galya	
20		Pentecaust		Archbishop of York; Vladimir Putin; David Lloyd George	Lightning; chivalry
21			2 billion years ago	US founders settlers;	
22	6th Day	Ascension		Stalin; East India Co.,	
23				Liberation movements; Einstein; Buddha; Georges Bataille;	DNA theory
24				Oliver Cromwell; Drake; BBC	Faith
25			2.5 billion years ago		Radio wave theory; Electromagnetic radiation; Hope;
26				John Lennon	Love
27	7th Day			Inner history of Church of England	Love of God
28				St John Baptist	
29		**When Christ leaves, my son and daughter become my leader on**		Son and daughter	Cycle times of sun; 30' tile of Earth axis;

		this pilgrimage			
30		Entry into Jerusalem		Pageant allegory of Church history	
31				Arrest and trial	
32			3 billion years ago	Crucifixion	
33		Pascha / Easter	15 billions years ago		

RESURRECTION

Ch	Place	Event	Era	People	Ideas / technology
1	Nowhere	Great Litany	No time	Leibniz, Newton, St Maximos	
2		Prayer of 1st Antiphon		Darwin, St Gregory the Great; **Galya**	Theory of explosives
3	A beach, Bardsey	First Antiphon		William of Orange; Ambrose of Medioloanum;	Charcoal, kiln fire; tolerance as first public virtue
4	Houses on the coast	Little Litany		Byron; Lincoln	Use of poetry
5	Hill station	Prayer of 2nd Antiphon		Kipling; Loyola; Ninian; St Gobain	
6	Sleep	2nd Antiphon		Newman;	
7	Morning	Little Litany		Holderlin	Motor and generator
8	Llyn, Clynnog fawr	Third Antiphon		St Beuno and St Winifred, GK Chesterton, Protestant martyrs	
9	Night	Prayer of Entry		John Chrysostom	Monarchy and two houses of commons and lords
10		Prayer of Trisagion		St Paul Apostle, St Makarios and Nikodemos	
11		Epistle		Dostoevski	Fire, explanation.
12	Dee Estuary	Gospel		Solzyhitsyn	
13	Walk south	Litany of Fervent Suppliation		William Law, Faraday	
14	Forest, heading for Llangollen	Prayer of Fervent Supplication		Shakespeare, Maxwell	
15	Bala	Litany of Departed		Nelson spoken of	
16	Boat on Dee,	Litany of Catechumens			

	Llan, Abbey			
17		Prayer for Catechumens	Pascal and a green man	Oil extraction and refining
18	Dee and Holt	1st Litany		Heat and thermodynamics; engine and piston
19	Home, Chester	2nd Litany	Duke of Westminster	Crown and parliament
20	Foregate	Cherubic Hymn	Henry Vth	How to make glass
21	Cathedral	Great Entrance	King David; St Augustine of Canturbury; Lord Herbert of Cherbury; Thatcher	
22	Walk home	Litany of Oblation	St David of Wales, Parachute Regiment	
23	Home	Prayer of Proskomedia		Origins of heavier atoms
24		Symbol of Faith	Galya	
25	Night	Anaphora		Atomic nucleus and mass; male and female
26	Wrexham	Litany before Lords Prayer	Graves, Sassoon, David Jones, Geraint Jones	
27	Wirral	Lord's Prayer	James, brother of Lord	On the composition of the Gospels
28	Birkenhead	Elevation	Father Paul Elliot	
29	Liverpool	Holy Communion	Prof. Stephen Clarke	Biology, science, theology
30	Night, roadside	Distribution	Nana and Taid	
31	Home / Palace	Thanksgiving	Queen Elizabeth II	
32	Home / Whitehall	Prayer behind Ambo	Theotokos	
33	Home	Dismissal	Christ	